THE STORYTELLING SALESMAN

Enriching Tales for Better Business

JAMES "JIMMY VAN" VANDERLINDEN

◆ FriesenPress

One Printers Way
Altona, MB R0G 0B0
Canada

www.friesenpress.com

Copyright © 2024 by James "Jimmy Van" VanderLinden
First Edition — 2024

All rights reserved.

No part of this publication may be reproduced in any form, or by any means, electronic or mechanical, including photocopying, recording, or any information browsing, storage, or retrieval system, without permission in writing from FriesenPress.

This book is a memoir. It reflects the author's present recollections of true stories and experiences over time. Some names and characteristics have been changed, some events have been compressed, and some dialogue has been recreated.

ISBN
978-1-03-919547-9 (Hardcover)
978-1-03-919546-2 (Paperback)
978-1-03-919548-6 (eBook)

1. BUSINESS & ECONOMICS, E-COMMERCE, INTERNET MARKETING

Distributed to the trade by The Ingram Book Company

TABLE OF CONTENTS

Introduction 1
Foreword 3
1. If You've Got Time to Lean, You've Got Time to Clean ... 7
2. Knowing Their Worth—and Your Own 17
3. Foresight and Burning Bridges 29
4. Respect Must Be Earned, Not Expected 43
5. Motivation: How to Achieve It, How to Kill It 51
6. Taking the Plunge: Starting a Business 57
7. Shenanigans: Go with Your Gut 69
8. Working from Home: It Ain't Always Great 75
9. Know the Law: When Success
   is Followed by Empty Threats 79
10. Juggling Good Ethics and a Good Income 85
11. Banks: You Hate Them But You Need Them 101
12. Keep It Lean 107
13. The Coach Doesn't Congregate with the Players 113
14. Interviews: Seeing Through the Bullshit 125
15. Pay Everyone Else Before You Pay Yourself 135
16. Knowing When to "Eat Shit" 143
17. Money Out > Money In = Bad 149
18. When It's Time to Cut the Cord 161
19. What's the Benefit? 173
20. Selling the Business: Reality vs. Fairy Tale 177
21. When the Money is No Longer Enough 181
References 193
Acknowledgments 197
About the Author 201

INTRODUCTION

I'VE NEVER BEEN A FAN OF "SELF-HELP" ANYTHING: NOT BOOKS, not videos, not seminars, nothing. But I do enjoy a good story.

Maybe more so than that, I enjoy *telling* a good story. In fact, on a weekly podcast I do for Fightful.com on Wednesdays, called *Fightful's The Hump,* whenever a topic sparks a relevant tale out of me, our viewers joke that it's time for "Storytime with Jimmy." And for some reason, I have a lot of them from my professional life that I've remembered, and many of them are actually pretty good.

Often when dealing with new staff or colleagues or even with long-time employees, I'll recall a story from my past to help explain whatever point I'm trying to get across. And it wasn't unusual for someone to suggest that I write a book to share these business-related stories.

So, who is this book for? It's for anyone who manages a business or manages people—or aspires to one day. It's for anyone with an idea for their own business but no experience of where to take it, let alone the pitfalls along the way. It's for anyone who already has a business, but it's not meeting their expectations, and they're ready to explore change whether it be to their people or to their process. It's for anyone grinding away at their job who's looking for tips on how to make their situation better.

And maybe most of all, it's for anyone who likes a good story.

I am not a life coach. I am not a motivational speaker. You will not see me in an infomercial promoting a seminar. I'm just a regular guy who has spent a lot of years in the business world, saw and experienced a lot of the good and the bad, and has a knack for recalling those experiences whenever a situation calls for it.

So sit back, put your feet up and enjoy! These stories are all true, and I hope you find them interesting and even funny. And who knows, maybe you'll learn something along the way that will help you in your professional journey as you go about creating stories of your own.

FOREWORD

by Sean Ross Sapp, Managing Editor, Fightful.com

JIMMY VAN CHANGED MY LIFE.

There are a handful of people I can say that about, who are not a member of my immediate family. Sure, there are people that have helped along the way for brief periods—professors who gave valuable lessons—but those were for fleeting moments in time. Jimmy Van helped change my life, my future, and the life of my family.

I was a successful yet struggling professional wrestling writer in 2016. I'd just released my first prominent feature, was on a heavily watched podcast, and the number-two writer on the most visited wrestling news website on the planet. Even though I was making next to nothing, after years of making literally nothing, I felt there was a future there.

There wasn't.

I'll never forget asking for a pay bump to $1,500 a month at that place so I could afford bills in a crumbling house, in one of the cheapest places to live in the country. I was turned down. I had to bet on myself, but fortunately, Jimmy was willing to bet on me. He had an idea to change the line of work I was in and wanted someone with a matched passion.

The website that rejected my raise has since attempted to bring me back and tried to entice three of our staff members to lead the charge. It's an endorsement of Jimmy Van's ability to see what people see in themselves and make it a possibility. I've heard of him giving people opportunities because they made him laugh while serving him food. I've seen him give people opportunities both in and out of their wheelhouse and help them shine.

Other things that Jimmy made a possibility: my family traveling out of the country for the first time, buying my first home, and helping to cover my wife's medical bills that came up in a time of emergency. Things you won't read about in this book or hear us talk about on the air.

Jimmy is a man who has built himself across multiple industries as a remarkable success. You'd never know that when you see him in his cargo shorts, his $20 Lugz shoes—I'm not convinced they still make those; I think he just bought out the stock—and a hat from a company he owns.

One of the most satisfying things about doing business with him is to witness his visions come into focus and enabling other people to see theirs through, and how they match up or differ.

I'll give you an example. We started Fightful as a completely free website, which led to some monetization issues. Jimmy wanted to institute a paywall for our exclusive content to develop a community within a community. Within a few years, we were the largest wrestling property in Patreon history times three. I wasn't on board with that, he was. I saw it through, and it worked wonderfully for us. This has happened the other way around as well.

An important lesson (that I SOMETIMES employ) I've learned was, "What's the benefit?" An oft-recited line—probably to me more than others. This applies to time versus money, social media etiquette, or really anything. Sometimes emotion prevails, but the line is always in my head!

I've also had the benefit of meeting Jimmy's family, his friends, his colleagues, and his employees. The people he's surrounded by reflect that personality, generosity, success, and dedication. The passion that I mentioned above, when matched, he recognizes that. In life, business, or in general.

Sean and I prior to doing an in-studio taping of our "The List & Ya Boy!" podcast for Fightful, now known as Fightful's The Hump.

1

If You've Got Time to Lean, You've Got Time to Clean

MOST OF US WORKED SOME KIND OF JOB IN OUR YOUTH, WHETHER IT be delivering newspapers, or working fast food, or mowing lawns, or running a lemonade stand in the driveway. You might think back to those days and laugh at how little you were paid for your efforts. But when I think about my first job, I'm appreciative for the work ethic it helped instill in me.

I was sixteen years old when I got a job working at a donut shop at a truck stop off the highway near my house in a small Canadian town. I was at the age where my wants exceeded my allowance, and I didn't want to rely on handouts from my parents, which would never have been enough to pay for all the material possessions teenagers desire anyway. I needed to earn my own money, and so this afforded me the chance to do that.

As is common in the fast-food industry, teenagers were prevalent among the workforce at my shop since the minimum wage was $8 an hour in 1990 in Ontario, Canada, with no benefits. A lot of teenage employees meant a lot of turnover, especially at the start of each new school year.

The shifts could be grueling and hard for anyone to endure, let alone a kid my age. And I still remember dreading every holiday weekend—even though we earned extra pay on those days—because the tour buses would come in and the place would be a madhouse, with people ignoring the lines and crowding around our counters trying to all order at the same time.

16-year-old me working my first job at a donut shop.

I spent two years working at that shop, including full-time summers and part-time during the school year, choosing to quit before my senior year of high school so that I could focus on my studies heading into university. Or so I claimed—of course that was bullshit. I didn't focus on school any more than I ever did, I just didn't feel like working there anymore.

And I'm sure, like every other kid, I was probably overcome with joy on my last day knowing that I would no longer have to put on that uniform and work that job ever again. But in retrospect, getting that opportunity was one of the best things that ever happened to me and it put me on the path towards financial independence years later.

Prior to working at that shop, I had witnessed on a regular basis what work ethic was truly like in the form of my mother, Tina.

My parents were European immigrants who owned a grocery store when I was a kid, and in fact my father was an entrepreneur who always found ways to make money and never worked for anyone else since before I was born, despite only completing the 5th grade in the Netherlands and moving to Canada at the age of twenty-nine, unable to speak English.

But while my dad Cornelus had hustle and business sense, what he didn't have was any interest in manual labor whatsoever. That meant that the grunt work was left up to my mom, and she delivered in spades with never a complaint.

My father Cor and mother Tina at the grand opening of their grocery store.

For years, my mother worked in the store full-time while also managing the staff and the business, on top of taking care of my sister and me, plus my dad, our house, our pets, and the yard work. She was a machine, and after they sold the store, she continued to take care of all the house and yard work herself, well into her seventies, until she finally acknowledged that she needed to hire some help.

I would lovingly call Mom "The Beast" because that's what she was in terms of work ethic and getting tasks done. But even though I witnessed her elite level of productivity every day, it never rubbed off on me in my youth, and I opted to spend most of my time laying around watching TV or playing video games. That is, until I started that job at the donut shop.

Each day when I would walk into work, I'd cross my fingers hoping that I'd be assigned to kitchen duty as opposed to the front counter.

In the kitchen, employees weren't customer-facing, and so they had a lot more leeway in terms of slacking off and killing time. If I were lucky, I'd be put in charge of food preparation—making anything from cookies to muffins to croissants to sandwiches—or donut preparation, meaning I'd put toppings on donuts or fill the stuffed donut holes or whatever.

The food-prep job is what everybody wanted because the work wasn't boring or tedious, and the shifts went by fast. But the tenured staff typically grabbed those positions, and more times than not I worked the front counter. And when you're talking about a busy shop off the highway where there would frequently be a barrage of customers, I drew the short straw whenever I had to work the counter. It wasn't uncommon for me to return home after a shift with sore feet, baggy eyes, and a uniform covered in powdered sugar and coffee stains.

My direct manager's name was Marion. All these years later, I still remember her for something she used to frequently say: "If you've got time to lean, you've got time to clean."

On front-counter duty, the second half of the evening shift was typically peaceful once the dinner rush ended, as was the first half of the morning shift before the lunch rush began. And as much as I hated starting work at 7:00 a.m. as a sixteen-year-old, I at least knew I could take it easy for a few hours before lunch. But not if Marion was there.

Often it felt like she worked stealth.

I'd finish up with a customer, there'd be nobody else around, and so I'd take a deep breath and lean against the back counter. Next thing I knew, I'd hear it: "If you've got time to lean, you've got time to clean," she'd say. Sometimes I'd try my luck and respond with something like, "I already cleaned the countertops Marion," but she'd be quick to answer with an alternative task like, "Have you wiped down the tables?" or "Have you swept the floor?" or "Get some ice and salt and clean the coffee pots." (which really works by the way). She insisted that we keep busy, and in turn, she instilled in us a good work ethic whether we wanted it or not.

In my mid-twenties, I taught myself how to build a rudimentary website using the old Geocities service that paved the way for website builders like Wix.com years later. I created a site about one of my childhood passions, professional wrestling.

This was the late 90s—there was no Meta (Facebook) or X (Twitter) or TikTok or YouTube, and Google was in its infancy. That meant that my site had much less competition for eyeballs and so while I hadn't intended for it to become a full-time venture when I started, that's what it turned into as my traffic numbers grew and I learned more and more about selling my own advertising banners on the website.

I decided to go for it, quit my day job at the time—selling job-search VHS tapes to schools and libraries, which is a whole other story in itself—and put my full-time effort into my website. But then the dotcom bubble burst in 2001, and my ad rates were slashed by 90 percent month-over-month.

I could no longer sustain a full-time living through my site. But I also wasn't ready to throw in the towel either. And so that work ethic that my mother and Marion had both instilled in me as a teenager came into play.

I started looking for ways to supplement my income while continuing to put full-time hours into my site, waiting and hoping for the ad industry to recover.

I spent hours scouring the Internet for opportunities and ended up doing everything from freelance writing for other sites, to web design and maintenance for a small American pro wrestling company, to customer support for an online casino, to handling pizza delivery phone orders—which I didn't realize is mostly done from home. All the while I kept working full-time on my site, and there were weeks that I was putting in eighty hours of work combined between different jobs.

I still have a vivid memory of a girl I was dating at that time coming to visit and sitting on my couch alone for hours while I sat at my computer trying to finish a freelance article before deadline because I needed that payday. I remember her openly sighing and continually asking me when I'd be done, because she'd spent her whole day at her job and simply wanted to relax and watch a movie with me. But unbeknownst to her, whether I could afford groceries the following week was dependent on me hitting that deadline.

I have another memory involving the same girl—this time we were startled awake early one Saturday morning by a phone call from a collection agency inquiring about a payment on my credit card debt. I hung up and told her it was a wrong number, but I'm pretty sure she'd heard the caller speaking and knew the truth. It was an embarrassing moment, but it's a moment I learned from because it made me want to work even harder and do better.

My first job at that donut shop taught me about work ethic, and it taught me about the value of a dollar.

To this day, I'd rather spend $25 on a pair of discount sneakers than $200 on a pair of Jordan 1s regardless of how much is in my bank account. And I have nothing but respect for those who work in the food service industry, because I understand what a grind it can be and the hustle and patience that are required to be successful in that business.

Financial freedom comes through work and perseverance. Unless you win the lottery, nobody is going to just hand you anything. If you've got time to lean, you've got time to clean.

LCF: The Opportunity Killers

If you have an idea for a business, it's unlikely that anyone is going to approach you on the sidewalk, hand you a big check, office space, personnel resources, and say "GO!" You must have the ambition, the drive, and the motivation to create your own opportunities.

From my experience, there are three main "opportunity killers" that you must make sure don't creep into your life and prevent those opportunities from coming to fruition. I call them LCF: Laziness, Contentment, and Fear.

Laziness. You're not happy with your current situation. You want more. More money. More professional growth. But after a long day of work, the last thing you want to do with your evenings and weekends is to work even more and put time and effort into something with no guarantee of a financial payoff, whether it be a new job search or a new business idea. Instead, you want to kick back on the couch, watch TV, play some video games, and maybe catch up on your sleep. And so the days turn into weeks, the weeks turn into months, and you remain unhappy.

Contentment. Again, you're not happy with your current situation and want more money and growth opportunities. But you know what? Your place of work is pretty laid back. You know all your co-workers, you like them, you might even consider them friends. You allow that contentment to trump your desire to do more and to make more, and as a result you watch as others pass you by.

Fear. You want to move on from your current situation, but what happens if it doesn't work out? What happens if you leave your current job to start your own business, run out of money, and end up unemployed when you have bills to pay and a family to support? Or what if you find a new job but end up getting fired? What if, what if, what if.

Two years. That was the timeline I always put on myself with any job. I would commit to two years and after that I would consider how much money I was making as well as opportunities for advancement. If I was happy with the money, happy with the work environment and saw opportunities for growth, I would commit to another year. But if I wasn't happy with what I saw, I would find a new job and move on.

I stuck to that two-year rule my entire working life as an employee, and I never allowed LCF to get in the way of that.

Life is all about taking chances. You'll never get the girl (or guy) if you don't at least approach them. You'll never lose weight if you don't adjust your diet and/or exercise routine. And you'll never succeed in business if you allow one or more of these opportunity killers–LCF–to creep into your life.

Sometimes work gets challenging, and you think there's no light at the end of that tunnel, but I've always believed that if you put in the effort, everything will work out in the end. So get off the couch. Get out of your comfort zone. Stop thinking about the worst-case scenario. And get to work.

2
Knowing Their Worth– and Your Own

IF YOU'RE AN EMPLOYER OR MANAGER, TAKE CARE OF YOUR MOST valued and most trusted employees. If you try to nickel and dime them just to pad your own bottom line, eventually you will regret it. And the time and cost associated with replacing them could prove to be immeasurable.

And if you are a productive employee, you wield a lot more power than you might think. Know your worth.

I'll never forget the years that I spent working for Yahoo Canada starting in 2002, which at the time was a major Internet company. I had been waiting for the ad industry to recover following the 2001 dotcom crash so that I could continue operating my own website full-time, but it hadn't happened, and I needed a job.

By this point, I was twenty-eight years old, hadn't had a real office job in several years and hated the idea of having to compete with people almost ten years younger for entry-level positions. But I'd taught myself how online advertising worked, and so that seemed like a logical industry to jump into and one that I thought could end up being lucrative for me.

I was hired as a Credit & Collections Analyst for a job-search website called HotJobs, which was a subsidiary of Yahoo. I handled credit applications on new accounts as well as collections and debt repayment. I made a small salary, however, there was a monthly bonus tied into the collection of aging money, and when I started the job, the accounts were a mess, so at least I had the opportunity to make extra income that way.

I spent my days calling and e-mailing delinquent clients, sending them copies of invoices they supposedly hadn't received, reconciling payments, and handling credit reference checks on new accounts. Even though these were necessary tasks for the ongoing operations of the business, it didn't take long for me to realize the minimal value that management put on myself and my team.

In addition to the American collections group that I was part of, our office also housed a small sales team for the Canadian arm of HotJobs. Their revenue targets were miniscule compared to their U.S. counterparts, yet there was still much more importance placed on them driving new revenue than there was on my team collecting old money even though our accounts were usually a lot larger. It was common for that team to get catered meals or snacks in the boardroom while my team sat at our desks feet away, uninvited.

On one occasion, loud music started playing and alcohol started flowing in the middle of the afternoon, and there we sat expected to continue working. A friend of mine on that team recognized the unfairness of the situation and even brought a plate of catering treats to my desk. I eventually asked my manager, Aiden, if we'd be invited to the party, and when he indicated that we wouldn't, I shut off my computer and left for the day.

On another occasion, there was a large aging account from a major client worth six figures that had gone uncollected for many months. Co-workers before me had attempted to collect it and had failed, and so it ended up in my queue.

Given that the client was a major corporation, I knew there was likely a reason the balance hadn't been paid as opposed to them trying to simply skip out and run. So I asked the top boss of our division, Grayson, if I could get a certain bonus percentage on that account if I was able to collect, and he agreed.

After several weeks, a lot of phone calls and a lot of reconciliations, I got the balance paid in full. But every time I inquired with Grayson or Aiden about that bonus, I'd be told it was "pending approval" or "in progress" or some other excuse.

The bonus never came, and I eventually realized that they likely never intended to pay it to begin with. I should have got that bonus in writing but didn't—lesson learned.

One day, a co-worker and I were called into a meeting where we were told that we were being promoted. We would now be working for the parent company Yahoo U.S. directly instead of HotJobs, overseeing major money accounts.

We were also told that the parent company didn't pay monthly bonuses on collections the way HotJobs did, but not to worry, we would soon receive a raise in our base to compensate for losing our bonuses, plus we'd be eligible for stock incentives.

We were flown to Yahoo's headquarters in Sunnyvale, California, just outside San Francisco, a huge compound with all the amenities of a vacation resort. We got wined and dined, all expenses paid, and we met the whole team.

We were excited for this new challenge, not to mention the opportunity to earn a larger base and get company stock, and returned home from the trip with a renewed energy.

Standing in front of the Yahoo sign at their headquarters in Sunnyvale, California.

Time passed, and we took on our new roles. The company had offices in several major U.S. cities, and because of time zones, combined with the fact that our team was a group of two, we were asked to put in later hours to accommodate multiple offices and would occasionally be given a day off to make up for that extra time. All the while, we were making less money than in our previous positions, because the salary increases and stock incentives hadn't yet come.

We would ask, and we'd be told to be patient. Meanwhile we'd see our HotJobs colleagues, who we'd supposedly been promoted over, making more than us due to the monthly bonuses that they continued to receive while ours were discontinued due to our "promotion." To say it was a morale hit would be an understatement.

When you are an employee of a company, especially a productive employee who: i) doesn't like your job; ii) doesn't like your treatment by management; and iii) doesn't care if you lose that job, you'd be surprised how much power you can have. And that is what my mindset became. I was young, single, and living in a small apartment with minimal expenses, so that job didn't make or break me, plus I always believed that I could find something else.

Now it just so happened that there was a diner located directly next door to our office. And it just so happened that we were given a fifteen-minute break twice a day, which office staff would typically take once every morning and every afternoon.

I decided to consolidate those two fifteen-minute breaks into one thirty-minute morning break and started going next door to that diner for breakfast with a co-worker every day. If the weather was nice, we would sit outside on their street-level patio and raise our coffee cups to toast management as they walked by.

Before long, Aiden approached me to tell me that he'd been told by Grayson to have me stop taking the long morning break and go back to two fifteen-minute breaks a day. I proceeded to remind him that I still hadn't received the raise in my base salary or information on the stock plan as I'd been promised months earlier, and until I did, I wasn't interested in splitting up the breaks. Sure, maybe it was bold, and maybe I disrespected authority, but I'd been losing money for months at that point.

Finally, the big day came.

Management from company headquarters in California were coming to our little office in Canada to address our concerns about raises, since by that point most of the people on our team had been promised one for months and had yet to receive it.

We gathered in the boardroom, we asked the questions, and we were assured that finally, the raises would soon be handed out. Not long after that, we were told that one by one we would be called into a meeting with Grayson and informed of our raises.

Prior to our promotion, I had been making between $500 and $1,000 per month in bonuses based on the size of the accounts I was collecting on. That means that I'd lost upwards of $12,000 per year in income since I'd taken on the new role and stopped being paid bonuses. So I was expecting at least a $12,000 raise in my salary, if not more since I'd technically been promoted to a position that was supposedly a step up from my previous role.

The first person called in was my co-worker who had been promoted with me. He was given a $2,000 raise in his base. Not per month or per pay period, but a $2,000 raise in his annual salary. He was obviously upset as he would continue making less than he did with his monthly bonuses in his previous position, and the first words he muttered were, "Jimmy's not going to like this," in reference to me. I was the more outspoken one obviously.

So, Grayson decided to call me in next. He sat me down, and with a big smile he told me that I was receiving the largest raise of anyone in the office.

What Grayson didn't realize that I knew, was that my current salary was among the lowest in the office because I was part of the most recent group hired, and they had frozen pay increases since then. He proceeded to tell me that I was receiving a $6,000 raise in my annual base, which meant that like my co-worker, I would still be making less in my "promotion" than I had been previously when you factored in the bonuses, plus I'd still be among the lowest paid in the office.

I explained this to Grayson and reminded him that I'd been asking for the stock incentive paperwork to no avail. Grayson paused for a moment, and then without saying another word, extended a handshake to indicate that our meeting was over.

As far as I was concerned, my time with Yahoo was now also over.

After everyone had received their raises, we all went as a group to a nearby restaurant for a team lunch to be paid by the company. This is where I participated in an activity that in retrospect, maybe I should feel guilty about or feel was childish and unprofessional, but I don't because I know how much money I made that company, and I know how little they thought of my team and the disrespect we endured.

That day at that lunch, we participated in an activity that I was later told by co-workers was referred to by management as the climax of "The VanderLinden Era."

The establishment the company had chosen was a European marketplace style restaurant featuring various stations with different types of food such as steak, chicken, or seafood. When you entered the place, you were given an empty card. Then as you picked up food from a station, they would stamp your card with the food type and number of items you'd received. At the end of the meal, you would give your card to the server and be billed accordingly.

A couple of my disgruntled co-workers and I proceeded to go station-to-station taking full platters of food, whether it be a platter of smoked salmon, a platter of steak, whatever. We would bring the entire platter to our table, set it down, then without even taking a seat, we'd go to the next station and do it again.

By the end of the afternoon, we had likely spent a few thousand dollars between just a few of us.

But perhaps my most vivid memory of that day was when Aiden, my direct manager, came to me smiling, patted me on the back and asked me how happy I was with my raise. I told him that I would still be making less than I was pre-promotion and so I wasn't happy at all. His smile then disappeared, he looked me in the eye and said, "shame on you," and walked away.

I had established a two-year rule for myself with respect to any job. With two years having passed here, it was clear my only option was to move on.

I started applying for positions after hours and on weekends and would go for interviews during my lunch break. Before long I accepted a new job and gave the company my two-weeks' notice.

Then came *the* moment. The moment when I knew that the company had valued my work all along, despite the morning breakfasts and that infamous lunch.

Aiden called me into a meeting and told me that they wanted to give me a counteroffer for me to stay. But as had been the pattern the previous two years, their counter amounted to no more than another empty promise. I was offered a significant increase in my base in the form of a promissory note. Not an automatic immediate increase, but a promise to give me an increase at some point in the future.

It was an easy thing to turn down, and so I fulfilled the rest of my obligations and I left, never looking back.

I kept in touch with several people there, and some remain friends to this day. And so, I heard that within a year after I left, that office started to downsize, and everyone walked around on eggshells expecting to be laid off, which eventually they all were. Imagine if I'd bought into that promissory note?

I left Yahoo in 2004. In 2017 Yahoo sold most of its Internet business to Verizon Communications for $4.48 billion. Sounds impressive, but the company had once been valued at over $100 billion. (Goel 2017)

Following Yahoo, I started a job with AOL Canada. I wasn't yet in sales, which was my eventual goal, but fortunately I wasn't in collections either. I was an Account Manager, which was sort of an administrative type of role. Basically, I worked directly with the sales team. They would close an advertising deal, and I would set up the campaign on our online platform and manage the day-to-day, allowing the sales representatives to focus on prospecting new business.

I established good relationships with our clients and would help the sales reps close upsells on existing contracts or help close new deals. But unlike them, I didn't earn commission.

Eventually, some of my clients, and even a couple of my co-workers, suggested that I jump over to the sales team. It's something that I had thought about because I knew what they typically made in comparison to me, and so I was ready to make that move.

By 2006 I'd finished my second year at AOL. My two-year rule was in effect, and I wasn't content with my position or my income. I was also almost thirty-two at this point and needed to start making some real money. So, when I heard that an opportunity had opened to join the sales team, I went to my manager to express interest in it. She told me that I needed to go through the General Manager and that she would push for me if I wanted it.

Now it just so happened that our GM had previously been our Director of Sales, and he had interviewed me for my current position two years earlier, and so I knew him well. I met him on a couple of occasions about the sales job and expressed my desire to join that team, and he told me that he was open to the idea and would speak to my manager.

A few weeks later, a new guy strolled over to our department and introduced himself as the new sales hire. That was the moment I realized that the GM never seriously considered me for the role. Well, I was two years in and obviously didn't see the opportunity for advancement, so I started actively looking for a new position, landed my first ad sales job at a company called AZ Ads, and gave my notice.

For the next two weeks of my notice period, I would occasionally run into my GM in the lobby or walking down a hallway, and he would seemingly always dart off in a different direction and avoid me. Then on my very last day, he came over to my desk, told me he heard I was leaving, and that he wasn't happy that I was going to a competitor.

Now, AZ Ads was not a competitor of AOL, so I told my GM that. But even if they were, they gave me the opportunity that he wouldn't. After that came the obligatory "good luck" handshake, and that was that.

I was leaving a company that was a brand recognized worldwide, was well-funded and well respected, for a young company with none of that reputation or funding. But if I'd stayed, I don't believe I would have gotten the opportunity to jump to sales. And in retrospect, taking that new job put me on the path to starting my own business years later. And so, while I was sour on that GM at the time for not seeing any talent or value in me, I couldn't be happier about it now.

Remember how I said that Yahoo was acquired by Verizon in 2017? Well funny enough, two years before that, in 2015, AOL was also acquired by Verizon Communications meaning both AOL and Yahoo ended up falling under the same ownership. How ironic is that? (Rooney 2015)

Here's a side story again from my time with Yahoo that's worth telling.

I was once approached by a manager with the small HotJobs Canada sales team in our office. They offered me the opportunity to move over to their side of the company and become a sales executive.

I knew by that time that advertising sales was where I would eventually end up. But I also knew that that division was not where I wanted to begin my sales career. I knew all the reps on that team, I knew how inadequate the product was that they were being asked to sell, and I knew what a difficult time most of them were having with it. I wasn't interested and so I turned down the opportunity.

The next words from that manager, I never forgot, and I probably never will. They said, "Wouldn't you someday like to own a condo instead of renting?" Maybe if somebody says that to you, you'll take it differently. But I took it as someone—someone who didn't really know me, mind you—suggesting that I'd never be able to afford my own place if I didn't take that job. I remembered those words and used them as motivation.

When the end of that two years came, and I embarked on a new opportunity with AOL along with a new two-year timeline for myself, I added a new wrinkle to that timeline. Not only would I again look to move on in another two years if I wasn't content with my income and my position with my new employer, but I was determined to buy my own home by the end of that next two years. And I did.

3
Foresight and Burning Bridges

OFTEN PEOPLE LIVE IN THE PRESENT AND MAKE DECISIONS TO benefit them today without thinking about tomorrow. But you never know what someone you're working with today might be doing in five years and how they may be of use or even of need to you then. Even if you're the company veteran today, and someone else is the new rookie hire. You just never know. Kindness, respect, and professionalism in the workplace can pay dividends later just as rudeness, disrespect, and unprofessional conduct can come back to bite you down the road.

After leaving AOL I embarked on my first ad sales job in early 2006 when I was thirty-one, working for an online marketing company called AZ Ads. I was seated in a group of desks that included the veteran of the sales team, a person named Kayden. From my first day, he was anything but helpful and accommodating to me. In fact, he would basically ignore my presence and if he did speak to me, he was typically rude and abrasive. Never a hello. He would pass me in the hallway as if I wasn't even there.

Once when I was planning a company trip to Chicago, I landed a meeting with Dell computers, a potentially big deal. After I got off the call setting up that meeting, Kayden berated me in front of the others and told me about all the aspects of the call I'd done wrong. One of our co-workers pulled me aside later and told me that Kayden had tried to get a meeting with Dell for months and never could.

Kayden had a dedicated Account Manager who assisted him in setting up his campaigns. She was the type of person that you love as soon as you meet them. Just a beautiful, positive human being. On several occasions, I witnessed his mistreatment of her make her cry.

I vividly remember one such occasion. It was late afternoon on a Friday, and he put a stack of papers on her desk and told her to file them all away before she left for the weekend. She knew it would take her hours, and she broke down crying at her desk. I was new to the company, and he had tenure over me, so I kept my mouth shut—it's one of my professional regrets.

Eventually Kayden's behavior and treatment of others contributed to him being fired from that job. As fate would have it, I didn't stick around long either. I was asked to relocate to a company office in San Francisco. I wasn't interested in leaving Canada, and soon after I was laid off with about twenty other people.

Later that same year, in 2006, I got a sales job with another online marketing company called Incentaclick and over the next five years, I worked my way up to Director of the sales division. Meanwhile, from what I heard, Kayden bounced around between jobs, seemingly never able to stay at any one place for too long.

One day, my CEO came to me and offered me the role of General Manager, basically overseeing the day-to-day operations of the entire company. I was planning my exit at that point, so I turned him down. A short time later, he called me into his office and presented me with the résumé of none other than Kayden himself. He told me that Kayden was a candidate for the General Manager position and asked for my thoughts. I then very bluntly and honestly told my CEO that I should walk onto the sales floor, shut off the lights and computers, and send everybody home because the same thing would happen under Kayden, only I could do it in five minutes whereas it would take him six months.

In the end, I left Incentaclick to start my own business. And that CEO hired Kayden. Then, over the next several months, many of the top talent in that company resigned, in part because of Kayden's abrasive and abusive managerial style. Kayden ended up again out of a job, and the company eventually went out of business.

Fast forward several years, and one day out of the blue I got a message on Meta (Facebook) from Kayden. I now owned my own company, and he was interested in doing business with us. I guess it was no secret how I felt about him, and so he thought he should clear it with me first. I told him business is business, and he had my blessing.

I assigned Kayden's account to one of my senior account representatives and instructed him to monitor Kayden's account regularly to see if any revenue was generated. I suspected Kayden may have just been looking to get a login to our online platform so he could see our campaign portfolio and use us as a source of prospective leads he could solicit directly. After a month, Kayden's account had generated nothing, and so I had it shut down.

Here are a couple of other relevant stories about foresight and conduct.

During my years working at Incentaclick, I saw a lot of people come and a lot of people go. But I'm not sure I ever came across anyone quite like Dylan.

I still remember this well. We were on an airplane going to San Francisco for a conference. Most of the time the job required you to work in the office, and you'd spend all day at a desk soliciting new business through cold-calls or e-mails. But a few times a year, trade shows would be held in select cities, and it would give you the chance to meet colleagues and clients from the industry face-to-face. It was a great way to establish new relationships and solidify existing ones.

Our first, basic Incentaclick booth at an industry conference.
My future business partner Luke makes a cameo up front!

THE STORYTELLING SALESMAN

Dylan was new to the company working in sales, and I was the team veteran. While on the plane, he showed me a list of prospects that he was hoping to meet at that show. One of the names on his list was one of my active accounts—I guess they had a mutual friend. I told him that that was a current client of mine, meaning we were already doing business, and so he could take that one off his prospect list. He casually made note of it.

The first day of the show, we're standing at our company's booth on the conference floor. That client approached, and we started chatting. Dylan then immediately wedged his way between us and name-dropped the mutual friend to the client. That got them talking, and not long afterward, my boss told me that I'd have to transfer that account to Dylan.

Obviously, I wasn't happy and felt he'd pulled an underhanded tactic considering I'd told him on the plane beforehand that that was my client. But sales can sometimes be dog-eat-dog, especially when commission is involved. And I was doing well while he was new with no portfolio, so I let it go.

A few weeks went by, and another of my accounts began to dominate the charts with respect to daily sales. I was then told by someone in the office that Dylan was in the process of setting up the exact same campaign for a slightly higher rate through a broker.

In sales, you always want to work with the direct client—i.e., the owner of the product or service that you're looking to market—and not a broker or middle man, unless the direct client has an agency of record (AOR) that they want you to work with on their behalf, or unless you're looking for budget in excess of what you're getting directly. Working with the direct client can ensure you earn the highest rates and secure the biggest budgets, whereas a broker cuts into your margins and typically works with everyone, which makes it hard for you to maximize your budget with that client.

It appeared that Dylan was planning to intentionally work with a broker to get a tiny rate increase over my direct deal so that he could offer more to our traffic partners and subsequently shift the revenue and the commission over to himself from me on the same campaign.

Now, sales may have been dog-eat-dog and there were no formal rules against doing such a thing in our company, but it was generally frowned upon and not usually done. Everyone on the team communicated regularly and understood that that was a line you shouldn't cross. If one salesperson had a campaign directly and another salesperson found the campaign through a broker, they would typically inform their co-worker of it so that they could try to use it as leverage to increase their rates or budget with the direct client.

I decided to give Dylan the benefit of the doubt one more time and told him that I already had the campaign he was setting up, but I had it through the direct client, and so there was no need for the brokered deal. Dylan thanked me for the heads up. The next day he put the campaign live anyway.

I now believed that Dylan was the kind of person who would deliberately stab you in the back for his own financial gain. Well, I could be as cutthroat as anybody when I needed to be, and I had to preserve my client relationships and my income. So I had to retaliate.

I called my direct client, told him the story, and got a significant increase in the rate, easily trumping what Dylan had through the broker. But I decided to keep the news quiet until the next sales meeting, which is when everybody pitched their new campaigns.

Dylan went first, happily announcing that he had the biggest campaign in the company at a higher rate. I then let him know that I'd gotten a significant increase from the direct client, and so there was no need for his brokered campaign. A member of the traffic team, who we worked closely with and who would pitch our campaigns to our traffic partners, told Dylan in front of everyone that he hated pitching brokered campaigns, and so nobody in his portfolio would ever run it, especially at a lower rate than our direct deal. You could see the wind immediately come out of Dylan's sails.

By that point, Dylan's reputation with the team was, shall we say, less than stellar. And within a few months he left the company, and I never crossed paths with him again after that.

Were my actions harsh? Maybe to you they were, but not to me. It's like the old saying, "Fool me once, shame on you. Fool me twice, shame on me." I gave Dylan the chance to do the right thing, he chose the money, so I handled my business.

One of my teammates on the sales side was also a friend whom I'd helped get the job, an experienced, well-spoken salesperson named Gabriel.

Now Gabriel was the type who told it as he saw it. He could be confrontational and quick tempered and while I knew he had a good heart, it was his abrasive exterior that people often saw first. He subsequently developed a negative reputation with co-workers which ultimately cost him the job opportunity.

Gabriel could have been the top salesperson in the company and could have made a lot of money. But if one of his campaigns didn't perform as well as he had expected, his frustration would manifest itself in the form of snide remarks to the co-workers that he depended on.

I remember once when someone called out to him across the office to ask about a campaign. Before Gabriel could respond, another co-worker gave them the answer. That was enough for Gabriel to go off, dressing down that co-worker in front of all of us and reminding them that the first person had directed the question to Gabriel, not to them.

I once had lunch with a member of the traffic team, which the sales team worked with closely to generate volume on our campaigns. That team member said that they would rather make less commission than devote attention to Gabriel's campaigns. That sentiment was echoed by other members of that team, which was essentially the death knell for Gabriel's revenue prospects.

You can be the best at what you do. But you're only as good as your team and if you rub them the wrong way and lose their support, the repercussions will be obvious.

Over the years, I experienced several moments in which people who had disrespected me or treated me poorly as co-workers at other companies were suddenly e-mailing me looking to do business or even asking me for a job. There was something satisfying about that; about knowing that at one point in time I was dismissed as irrelevant to them, but now they needed something from me. But never did I offer employment to one of those people.

I've also had several occasions in which an employee who voluntarily quit my company, reached out either to me or someone else internally looking to get their job back.

You know the saying, "the grass is always greener on the other side"? Well, that isn't always the case. And unfortunately some employees discovered that the hard way after leaving for what they thought was a better opportunity elsewhere.

No office environment is perfect and I'm sure mine was no different. But we did our best to make everyone comfortable and to make everyone want to be there. I'd worked in enough offices to know that we'd done a pretty good job of it. And so my policy has always been to never allow anyone to return after they'd left voluntarily.

There was one notable exception. I had an employee who gave his notice, but he also gave me as great and as honest of an explanation as anybody ever could. He had recently gotten married, and he told me that he and his wife wanted to take a year to travel across the country before they settled down and began planning a family. He told me that his hope was that in a year's time, I would take him back. He was great at what he did and well liked by everyone, and I really respected his explanation. So a year later after he and his wife had returned home, I happily rehired him.

As mentioned, I've had colleagues over the years who didn't treat me well. But there have also been many who became friends. People who were always kind, always professional, and would reach out to say hello even if we weren't doing active business. I always make time for those people and whenever a relevant opportunity comes up, I always go to them first.

While working at AZ Ads, I met a gentleman named Riley. I didn't work with Riley on a day-to-day basis as we were in different departments, but I got to know him just by passing in the hallway or mingling at company functions.

After I left that company, and as time went by, I would bump into Riley at conferences, and even though we weren't actively doing business together, I would always make time for a drink and a chat with him. He was a good guy, a genuine person, and I considered him a friend.

One day Riley reached out to me out of the blue and asked me to lunch, so we met up at a local restaurant.

By that point, I owned my own business, and I hadn't seen Riley in a few years. He had long left AZ Ads by then as well. He told me that he'd been laid off from his most recent job a year earlier and had tried to go out on his own as a consultant, but unfortunately the opportunities weren't consistent, and he had a family to support. He wasn't asking for a job, he was simply looking to connect and thought maybe I would know of someone with an open position in his field.

Riley had gotten into an industry different than mine after we'd both left our old employer; he was in the market research space. Big brands are always looking to better understand their consumer base as well as economic trends to improve their bottom line. It's common now for brands to finance online surveys that ask consumers questions related to their product or industry in exchange for a reward such as a gift card or virtual currency. Riley had been working for a company that managed their own market research survey panel.

As he explained it, it sounded more and more like something I might want to explore. I had wanted to diversify my business and create multiple revenue streams, and this gave me a chance to do that and build a proprietary asset in the form of my own survey panel. So I said to Riley, how about I create a business unit in that niche, and you come work for me and head it up?

Together we built a proprietary digital platform that at its peak had tens of thousands of daily active users. All because Riley had decided on a whim to reach out, and because when I was the new guy at AZ Ads, he treated me with kindness and respect, and so he became someone I wanted to do right by and work with.

Dwayne "The Rock" Johnson has been quoted as saying, "It's nice to be important, but it's important to be nice." And from my experience, especially when it comes to business, he's right.

Now, having foresight shouldn't just pertain to actions involving attitude or honesty but also to general professional conduct. Sometimes a decision you make in the moment can have a negative impact later.

In 2001 after the dotcom bubble burst, and my website ad revenue plummeted, I took on various part-time jobs to make ends meet. One of those jobs had me doing customer service for an online casino. I worked the overnight shift on weekends out of their office, helping casino players with deposits, withdrawals, and general questions. I was in my twenties and single, so it's not like my Saturday nights were high-demand, and I needed the money.

Looking back, it's funny to me I took that job considering I'm not a frequent player of casino games aside from the occasional slots, yet there I was expected to answer detailed questions about Roulette or Baccarat.

One night, they were having an employee party for whatever reason. It was my work shift, so I sat at my computer servicing clients while the camaraderie went on around me. One of the web developers—I don't recall his name but I remember he was a friendly Eastern European guy—kept bringing me alcoholic beverages. And at first, I refused, because I was working. But he persisted, pressuring me to be a team player. So, I foolishly obliged him.

The next thing I remember is waking up on the floor of a bathroom stall the next morning. I was hungover, and I had apparently spent time vomiting based on the condition of the toilet. I checked the time, and my shift had ended. I knew instantly I would be fired.

I went to the office kitchen, and there were a few employees there starting their morning shift. They acted very awkward around me, and I'm sure my appearance was disheveled to say the least. They had a refrigerator where you could help yourself to refreshments, so I filled a small bag with cans of ginger ale because I was nauseated and again, I knew they were going to let me go. The next week, nobody called me. So, the following weekend I went back to work and within about ten minutes of my shift, I was called into the office and fired. My conduct was unacceptable, and I deserved it.

A few years later I was working at Incentaclick, and I was in Miami for a sales conference. I was with co-workers at the hotel, and one of them said that a friend of his from our industry who also lived in our town was going to come over. The friend walked in, I looked at him, he looked at me, and we instantly recognized each other. "Did you work for an online casino back in Toronto?" I asked him. He replied, "Yes ... are you the guy that got drunk at an office party?" Fortunately, we were colleagues and he laughed it off, but what if he'd been a decision-maker for a major client? I could have hurt our chances at closing that business over a stupid decision several years prior.

In October of 2015 the Toronto Blue Jays won their division in Major League Baseball for the first time in twenty-two years and were facing the Texas Rangers in the fifth game of a best-of-five playoff series, at home in Toronto. It was the night of the famous "bat flip" by Jose Bautista after he hit a three-run shot to win the game and the series for the home side.

At that point, I had owned my own business for four years. That particular baseball season, the Blue Jays had created a buzz not only in the city of Toronto, but across Canada. And that game five was a hot ticket. So, despite it being a weekday matinee game, we allowed our staff to have the afternoon off to either watch the game on television or go live if they had tickets. A dozen or so employees ended up getting seats, as did my business partner, Luke, and me.

A crowd shot from my seat at the 2015 American League Division Series, the night of Jose Bautista's infamous bat flip.

One of those employees was a relatively new sales hire named Dawson. In the short time he'd been with us, he'd already taken a few days off, plus we'd heard that he watched a previous Jays playoff game one afternoon on the television in Luke's office with his feet propped up on Luke's desk while Luke and I were out of the office. It's fair to say he was on thin ice with us.

We all had a great night due to the Jays winning, and some of us were out celebrating until the early hours. But the next morning, everybody showed up to work on time. Everybody that is, except Dawson. We called his phone, no answer. It wasn't until several hours later that he called back. He had just woken up after getting home late from a night of partying and went to sleep with clearly no consideration whatsoever for his job. We let him go that day and from what we heard later, he decided to join the military, which is probably exactly the sort of atmosphere and discipline he needed.

Sometimes it's difficult in the moment to have the foresight to think about how a decision you make now could impact you years later. But in these cases, we all should have known better. Kayden, Dylan, Dawson, and me—we should have known better.

The OPPOSITE of Building a Positive Reputation

That first sales job I had with AZ Ads was difficult in that they grouped us by territory.

Some members of the team worked the U.S. east coast or west coast, which was easy because most business resided in New York or California. The people working on those teams mostly sat around taking incoming calls all day, so it was an easy sell. But I was part of a group that handled the Midwest, and so Illinois and Michigan were your best shot at closing any decent business. It was a hustle, and I had to pound the phones all day with virtually no incoming calls to be had.

Wanda was one of the people assigned one of those major territories. She was always difficult to deal with and gave me attitude, and I recall her once complaining to our manager when I took a personal call at my desk. You know, *that* type. She had a negative reputation with several people in the office, even with some whom she considered to be her friends.

A couple of years later, when I was with Incentaclick, one of my accounts was a large dating website. Wanda came up in conversation with the client one day, because my contact was a former client at AZ Ads, and Wanda had been his sales representative there. He mentioned that he could really use help, like a marketing manager, and asked if I knew where Wanda was working because she'd left AZ Ads just as I had. I didn't know her situation, but it just so happened that her boyfriend at the time worked at my current company. So I told my client that I would inquire for him.

I asked the boyfriend, who said that Wanda was currently unemployed. He put me in touch with her, we had a conversation, and she expressed her interest in the job. I put her in touch with the client, and a little while later I found out that she'd been hired and would be our new day-to-day contact. But she never actually told me directly, rather her boyfriend did.

Then, it happened. My boss called me into his office, and he was smiling because he recognized the absurdity of the situation. He told me that Wanda had called him, had told him that she was our new contact on that account ... and that she wanted him to transfer the account to someone else instead of me. Yeah, that's right. She never thanked me for helping her get the job, and she never reached out after she took over the account, and so I never got any explanation. I just chuckled given her previous reputation, rolled my eyes, and that was it.

What more is there to be said except—don't be like Wanda!

4
Respect Must Be Earned, Not Expected

THERE'S A SAYING POPULARIZED BY A JANET JACKSON SONG—"WHAT have you done for me lately?" And those words speak volumes, particularly in business. Don't expect your staff to respect you just because you're their boss and you sign their checks. You need to command respect, not demand it. It needs to be earned. Regardless of your position within your company.

In my first advertising sales job with AZ Ads, my supervisor became somewhat of a mentor to me. Jack was a few years younger than me but had a lot more industry experience than I did, and his door was always open to answer questions and offer advice when needed. I liked him, and I respected him. He had earned that from me.

Years later I was with Incentaclick and had climbed the ladder to establish myself as the highest grossing member of the sales team. One of the company owners confided in me that they had an opportunity to hire a sales veteran who had left a competitor, and it was Jack. I was all for it. He treated me well in our time together, and so I vouched for him as a good hire.

Jack was hired and became my new direct boss. On his first day, he walked up to me and asked what time I'd gotten to work. Our office hours were typically 9:30 a.m. to 5:30 p.m. at that time, and it wasn't uncommon for me to arrive sometime before 10:00 a.m., one of the small perks that I'd earned with the owners by being a big producer. I responded to Jack that I'd gotten there around 9:45 a.m. He said, "9:30 you're on time, 9:31 you're late. Don't let it happen again," and he walked away.

Maybe it's just me, but I found that irritating. I'd been the top revenue generator there for a long time before Jack arrived, and that's how he chose to make his mark upon his arrival? I proceeded to tell one of the owners the story, and he said not to worry about it, everything was fine, and he'd talk to Jack.

Once a week we had a morning sales meeting, and the rule for that meeting was if you arrived at 9:31 a.m. or later, you had to buy coffee and donuts for the team. Typically, the correct time would be determined via our cell phones since the idea was, you can mess with a clock on the wall but not so much the mobile carriers. So, one morning I walked into the meeting with my phone showing the time of 9:29 a.m. Jack immediately declared that I was late. I pulled out my phone to show him that that was not the case, and he showed me his phone from a different carrier that showed a time a couple of minutes later. We carried on with the meeting and once it ended, we all went back to our desks, and Jack very loudly and abrasively told me to go get breakfast for the team.

Now I'll admit, I could be difficult at times and was never the type to back down, especially if I felt that someone was trying to embarrass me or show me disrespect. So, I refused and suggested that Jack go get breakfast. He then stood up at his desk, walked closer to me and repeated that I needed to go get the food. I held firm, said I wasn't late according to his own rules, and that if he wanted breakfast, he could go get it himself.

At that point, with the room so quiet you could hear a pin drop, I knew that Jack was out of options because the owners would never let him fire me given my production. So, after a few moments of silence, I yelled out—and I'll admit in retrospect, this was bold if not arrogant—"You know what, I guess you need the money more than I do, so even though I wasn't late, I'll be the bigger person, so breakfast is on me folks!"

Weeks turned into months, and Jack's reputation within the company deteriorated not just with me, and not just with co-workers, but with ownership as well. He would openly play online poker at his desk every day. He would have lengthy phone calls at his desk with his contractor discussing the specs on a new home he was building. He got drunk at a bar during a trade conference and made a scene in front of many of his co-workers and peers, causing him to have to apologize to our team the next day. And for whatever reason, he seemed to take pleasure in firing people, sometimes in front of all of us.

A lot of employees walked on eggshells fearing for their jobs. But that was a fear I never had, and admittedly I would use that fact to push Jack's buttons. I never knew the terms of his employment, but I'd heard that it was a one-year contract, because after about a year he was gone.

I believe that Jack made the mistake of thinking that because he was coming to our company from a long-time competitor where he had a managerial-level role, and because he was coming into a similar role with us, he would immediately command respect. I think that he believed he could display his authority over people and even talk down to them regardless of their tenure, and it was okay because of his job title. I don't think he understood that most of the staff at our company didn't know him, had never worked with him, and so to them, he was still the new guy. It didn't matter where he came from or what his job title was. He was the new guy. They reported to him, and so they would follow his orders, but his actions didn't do him any favors, nor win him any fans.

E-mail Marketing: Quality Over Quantity

Not only should you not expect to instantly command the respect of your staff based on who you are, but you also shouldn't expect to command the attention of a prospective customer based on the company you represent.

We live in a digital age in which sales solicitation has evolved from cold-calling and knocking on doors to prospecting business through e-mail and social media. We also have a lot of competition for eyeballs today with people having so many options with respect to how they spend their time. And so, sending out lengthy, detailed marketing e-mails will likely get your prospect to delete your message rather than reply to it.

When I first moved to Toronto and took a job selling job-search video tapes, it was the late nineties and the Internet wasn't as sophisticated or as widespread as it is today, and so the telephone was still the primary method that we used to generate new business. My boss gave me a long script and asked me to follow it on calls, and I hated it from the get-go. I felt it made me sound disingenuous, and I'm sure plenty of prospective clients were rolling their eyes as they listened along.

I ended up ignoring the script and tried to keep my sales pitch direct and personalized, and asked my prospects plenty of questions to get them talking and engaged in the conversation. My success rate increased as I evolved that method.

When I worked at Incentaclick, one of my bosses named Sebastian showed me e-mail templates and recommended I use them when sending out sales pitches to prospective customers. These templates contained several paragraphs with detailed information about the company, and it was overwhelming for me just reading them so I couldn't imagine how a client would feel. I again decided to ignore those templates and keep my pitch short and precise.

I would also try to personalize each message by looking for an applicable contact and addressing them by name as opposed to e-mailing a generic account like "info@" asking for "To Whom It May Concern." It was unlikely that those messages would end up anywhere aside from somebody's trash folder.

Customers want to know what you can do for them and how you can help them either save money or make money depending on what you're trying to achieve. When you're pitching them cold with no previous connection or referral, they don't care about your company, and you're lucky if they devote even ten seconds of their time to your message before they decide whether to move on. You need to speak their language and make it clear why they need to hear you out.

You also need to be patient and not bombard a prospective client. If you send them an e-mail every day, it's unlikely that they will respect your persistence. Instead, you'll probably annoy them and hurt your chances of ever closing that business. I would always rotate between e-mails and phone calls, one or two times a week tops.

I learned to do some research to try to turn an e-mail message from a cold unsolicited pitch to a warm one. If a company was currently working with one or more competitors, I would make sure I knew about it. I would try to find out what kind of sales numbers a prospective client was doing with a competitor and how much they were paying, in case there was an opportunity to save that customer money.

I would even try to find out some of the personal interests of the contact person.

Once, while at Incentaclick, I was trying to land the business of a large company, and the marketing contact just wasn't responsive. I happened to notice on their Meta (Facebook) page that they were interested in photography. So, the next time I sent them a sales e-mail, I personalized the message even more by mentioning photography and some of the locations they'd been to that I had also visited. That did the trick, I got a reply, and I closed that deal.

LinkedIn also became a valuable tool for me with respect to soliciting business. It's like Meta (Facebook) for professionals. And whenever you find a contact person there, it will tell you if you have any mutual connections, plus you can see the person's job history. I would use that to my advantage by mentioning a mutual connection in a message or mentioning any friends that I happened to have that worked at any of the same companies that they did.

Sometimes I would also reach out to the mutual connection and get them to introduce me, meaning my pitch wasn't cold anymore.

Today I get solicited a lot through e-mail and through LinkedIn, and I ignore almost all messages. One reason, as I've discussed, is that the messages are often way too long, too drawn out, and too impersonal. I also hate it when it's easy to tell that the sender was lazy and copied and pasted the same message to me that they likely sent to dozens of others.

Whenever I see a different font from one paragraph to the next, or two different sizes of font in the same message, I know that the sender put no effort into their work and did a basic copy and paste. If you don't care enough about me to at least make it look like you wrote the e-mail, then I don't care about your business.

Quality over quantity, and personal over generic—that is the recipe for success in the world of unsolicited sales messaging. Keep it short, precise, and make the customer care.

———■———

5
Motivation: How to Achieve It, How to Kill It

IF YOU'VE EVER BEEN AN EMPLOYEE AT A COMPANY, THEN YOU should have some idea of how to properly motivate a team. It's important to keep people happy and keep them incented to maximize their output. Conversely, if your team isn't motivated, that could impact their productivity and subsequently your company's profitability.

I'm sure we've all had a job in our lives in which management came up with an idea intended to provide motivation that they thought was brilliant while everybody else thought it was silly and hated its existence.

When I worked for Yahoo, the small HotJobs Canada sales team in our office had to hit a gong whenever they closed a deal, and then everybody would clap for a moment. My division in that office had a bell—a tiny, whimpering little bell that management wanted you to ring whenever you collected on an account.

I hated that bell, and I refused to ring it. Others in the office felt the same way, and a co-worker even stuffed paper towels into it once so that it barely made a sound when you hit it.

People did not look forward to hitting the gong or ringing the bell. It did not motivate them. In fact, it had the opposite effect—people dreaded having to take the stroll up there to ring that bell. But management, which was too far removed from the "trenches" in the office, had zero clue how to motivate their staff, and so to them it was a great idea.

That brings me to Jack, my former boss at Incentaclick. One of his first ideas after coming aboard was to introduce his own gong to our sales floor. But whereas the gong at HotJobs was a legitimate giant gong that you hung up, Jack's gong was a small table-top model. He proudly brought it to a sales meeting and indicated that every time you close a deal, you hit the gong.

Everyone on the team hated the idea, and because my relationship with Jack had started to deteriorate at that point, I was probably the most vocal in my disdain for this gong. But I decided to take it up a notch and play a little prank.

When Jack went out for his lunch break that day, I took the gong off his desk and put it in a drawer of an empty desk nearby. As Jack returned from lunch, I stared at my monitor looking focused while using my peripheral vision to see what would happen next. Jack noticed the missing gong as he approached his desk and stopped in his tracks. He then looked over in my direction but said nothing, likely suspecting that I was the culprit.

For the rest of the afternoon, not a word was spoken about that gong. But at the end of the workday as Jack was getting ready to leave, his curiosity got the best of him. He strolled over to my desk and sighed, "Okay, what did you do with the gong?"

I gave him a puzzled look as if I didn't know what he was talking about, and said, "Why, what happened to the gong?" I claimed I didn't know it was missing, and he begrudgingly left for the day.

After he left, I took the gong out of the empty desk and put it back in its original place. I never saw that gong again, and so I can only guess that Jack came to figure out that it wasn't a successful effort.

Was I a jerk for hiding the gong? Maybe. But nobody liked it, it didn't motivate anyone, and I didn't feel that simply telling Jack that was going to be enough to change his mind.

The first holiday season that I was with AOL Canada in 2004, they gave everybody a blanket with their logo embroidered on it as the annual holiday gift.

In the days and weeks prior, we had all talked amongst ourselves about what kind of holiday bonus we could expect that year. Suffice it to say, we were hoping for some sort of financial reward. And so those blankets were not well received even though management presented them with big smiles and talked about how beautiful they were. Kind of like Clark Griswald getting his "Jelly of the Month Club" voucher in the movie *Christmas Vacation*.

I remember that evening. As a bunch of us walked down the street carrying the boxes containing our blankets, one of my co-workers gave his to a homeless person. I ended up giving mine to my parents. I'm sure the company mass-produced those blankets, and they didn't cost much. But whatever the cost was, we would have still been happier with the cash equivalent than with those stupid blankets.

Hitting a gong is not a proper means of motivation. Bringing in free bagels once a quarter won't do it either. People want to know that their work is appreciated, and they want to know that more opportunities and more incentives will come their way if they do a good job.

I was always aggressive with the commission plan I gave my sales team because I wanted them to be motivated to earn as much as they could, which would in turn make more money for the company.

If a new position opened, I would look at any promotions and lateral moves I could make internally first before recruiting someone new. I did "Employee of the Month" awards that came with a $500 gift card, and I would always choose non-commissioned staff for that award. During the holidays every year, I gave each employee a $500 gift card as a bonus. If people contractually had three weeks of vacation time per year but were good performers and asked for additional days, I'd give it to them.

Salary increases, a new job title, the opportunity to learn new skills or take a course paid for by the company—these were the kinds of moves that I made as an employer, and I believe it's a big reason why our turnover was always low, and people typically wouldn't leave unless we told them to.

People do not go to work for you because they want a social life. They do it to make a living. And they don't stay with you for a long period of time out of loyalty, or at least most don't. They stay because of how they're treated, how they're compensated, and the environment that you've created for them. That is how you motivate.

Here's a great story about the importance of a good work environment.

I once hired an entry-level sales representative who had previously worked as a bank teller for a major financial institution. He wanted the job at least in part because he was tired of the corporate bureaucracy that comes with working in that kind of environment. I think the fact he could get away with a T-shirt and blue jeans in the office was also a bonus.

On a routine basis, this kid would contact me on Instant Messenger during the workday to ask me for permission to use the bathroom. Eventually after about a week of this, I called him into my office. I asked him why he felt the need to ask permission to go to the bathroom. He explained that at his previous job because he was dealing with customers as a teller, he could never leave his post without asking for permission first and so it had become a habit.

My response made him smile. "Well, this isn't *Shawshank Redemption*," I said. "When you need to go take a piss, just go take a piss."

6
Taking the Plunge: Starting a Business

IT SEEMS EVERYONE DREAMS OF OWNING THEIR OWN BUSINESS. Being the boss, calling the shots, having financial freedom. Sounds great, right? It's not as easy as you think. It takes time, planning, and capital to make it work. And even then, there are no guarantees.

According to *Exploding Topics*, 10 percent of new businesses don't survive their first year. And in years two through five, a staggering 70 percent of new businesses will fail. (Howarth 2023) But that didn't enter my mind back in 2011 when, after having spent five years with Incentaclick and working my way up to Director of Sales, I felt the next logical step for me was to start my own company in the same industry.

I'd seen a lot of change since I'd started there five years earlier. The founders of the company had sold it to a small public firm. And as often happens, new management brought in their own people to fill executive positions in an industry that they had no experience in. I learned a lot about how not to run a business from that point forward. And as time went by, bad decisions were made, and revenue subsequently declined. Cash flow became a problem, and our traffic partners—who were key to generating sales—were getting paid late or not at all. We started to establish a negative reputation within the industry, and I realized that the longer I stuck around, the more that reputation could impact me.

If your goal is to start your own business, the first thing you need to determine is, is your idea a legitimate business, or a pastime? You might read that and think, what do you mean, of course it's a business! But do you know how your idea is going to make money? Do you have a business plan? What will your starting costs be like? What's the profile of your customer? Who are your competitors? If you can't answer all these questions, then at this stage, you've got yourself a pastime.

Once you've established your business plan, your next step will probably be to decide on a name for your company. I would always scour the Internet to make sure that any name I chose wasn't already taken in the same industry and that the domain (i.e., the dotcom name) was available.

We live in a digital world, and your online presence is of the utmost importance. The last thing you want is to choose a name for your business that is already taken in terms of the web domain. You'll limit your word of mouth and inadvertently send free traffic to the other guy's website.

The same idea applies to the name of your handle on the various social media channels. If @"yourname" is already taken across the major platforms, it might be a wise idea to pivot and think of a different name.

Our first business name was Oasis Ads, and I came up with that after brainstorming at my kitchen table and glancing over at a carton of Oasis orange juice. Sure, the beverage company had the domain Oasis.ca, and Oasis.com was taken as well but there was no company in our industry with Oasis in its name, and "Oasis Ads" didn't exist, so we were able to register the domain and social media accounts with no issue.

We also wanted to create a parent company name because we eventually wanted to build multiple divisions and not just an online marketing company, so the idea was Oasis Ads would be one subsidiary of the parent.

While working at Yahoo, my eventual partner and I would jokingly use the phrase, "All wrong, don't care," to describe some of the nonsense we experienced at that job and our lack of incentive and motivation. We ended up shortening that phrase to "AWARE" to create our parent company name, Aware Ads.

Various logo concepts we went through before picking a winner for our company. The little details are important.

Once you decide on a business name, you'll likely have to determine how much capital you'll need to get started and whether you have enough. It's very common in the business world for people to get together with friends and/or family members, pool resources, and go in as partners. And if you came up with the business idea together, then of course you're going to partner up and take this journey towards financial freedom and success together, right?

Now on the surface, this sounds like a no-brainer. You'll have someone to share in the expenses and the workload. You'll have someone you can bounce ideas off of. And you'll have someone to share the responsibility for business loans, or office leases, or anything else that comes along. But don't lose sight of the fact that deciding to go into business with a friend or family member is a very important decision that should not be taken lightly.

I started my company in a 50/50 partnership with one of my best friends and former co-workers from Yahoo, AZ Ads, and Incentaclick, a guy named Luke. I did so because we both had experience in the online marketing industry, and I did so because I needed help getting started financially.

I knew that Luke was a little rough around the edges and had jumped around from job to job in the years before we started the business, whereas I had maintained the same position for years. But I trusted him and knew he wasn't the type that would decide one day to drain the bank accounts and run. Still, I went through the process the proper way and had a lawyer draft a shareholders' agreement that outlined all our rights, and all our responsibilities. Friends or not, this was business, and Luke had no problem with it.

As the years went by, I habitually took the lead on almost all day-to-day matters in our business. I did so because it was in my nature to take charge, and I did so because I felt that if I left certain tasks up to Luke, they might sit on the backburner and not get done in a timely manner. Everything from finding office space, to negotiating the lease, to hiring contractors and overseeing the renovation of that space, to getting office furniture, to dealing with our lawyers and accountants, to recruiting and hiring staff, to doing payroll, to exploring and launching new business opportunities and ventures, to monitoring the bank accounts, credit cards, cash flow and accounts receivable—all of it went through me.

Sometimes a client or colleague didn't even know I had a partner until they'd come into the office or to a trade show and meet Luke. And I'd be lying if I said that there weren't some quarters when I would cut our dividend checks and be bothered by the fact that we were getting paid the same when the output ratio wasn't the same. I complained to Luke a few times about the size of my workload versus his, and he would encourage me to hire help. But I dealt with a lot of sensitive, if not confidential, company information and wasn't overly comfortable delegating much of that work.

On the bright side, we had seen dozens of other companies in our space disintegrate because of a falling out between the partners, but that never happened with us. We had heard the horror stories of how one partner would clear out the cash in the bank, or cut side deals for himself, or abuse their expense account on high-priced frivolous matters, or be an absentee owner who never showed up to work. None of those issues ever entered our workplace.

Is every partnership going to be perfect? No. Was mine? Certainly not. Luke would, on occasion, make a promise or a decision with an employee and not inform me of it, meaning I'd have to hear about it after the fact from somebody else. And he sometimes would leave early and not let me know, meaning again I'd have to hear about it from someone else. And because he was a little rough around the edges, he would sometimes send a division-wide or company-wide e-mail or Instant Message (IM) that he thought was funny, but that others could have deemed offensive and potentially held us liable.

You might be asking yourself—did I ever consider dissolving the partnership and moving on? The answer is no. Luke oversaw a side of the business that I wasn't interested in managing. Plus, I knew I could trust him. And he was a good sounding board for me. We were on the same page with respect to decision-making almost all the time, and whenever we did disagree, we were able to resolve matters easily.

Besides, I know I wasn't the greatest partner all the time either. I can be stubborn or want tasks to be done my way. I can be loud, I can be outspoken, and sometimes I'm very blunt. Nobody's perfect, and that certainly includes me.

Matter of fact, we think that I inadvertently contributed to Luke getting fired from Incentaclick! I knew management didn't like that we were friends and had concerns that we'd one day leave to start our own company—which we did many years later. They eventually let him go and we've always believed that our friendship was the reason. We can joke about it now!

With Luke and another friend Kelvin at the NHL Stanley Cup playoff game between my beloved Edmonton Oilers and the San Jose Sharks in 2017.

No matter how much you trust or even love your new prospective business partner, understand what you're getting yourself into if you go into business with them. Understand that they will be expected to put in the same number of hours and effort that you do, and that if they don't, you have little recourse unless you want to dissolve the company and make it ugly, potentially destroying your once close relationship.

Understand that if you go 50/50, they will earn the same income that you do regardless of who's doing the most work, who's cutting the best deals, or who's coming up with the best ideas. And understand that if you don't go 50/50, and there's a majority owner, the one with the minority stake will likely at some point feel underpaid, undervalued, and entitled to more money, whether they are or not.

Ah yes, money. Those who don't have it, want it. And those who do have it, want more. Financial freedom is a source of pride, it's a source of comfort, and it's a source of power. It can also be a reason for betrayal. We've all heard stories of friends, colleagues, and family members turning their backs on their loved ones over money. Even in the Bible, according to the Gospel of Matthew 26:15, Judas betrayed Jesus in exchange for thirty silver coins. Money changes relationships, and the more successful you become, the more cognizant of that fact you need to be.

How many times have you heard stories on the news about someone who regretted winning the lottery because it changed the way their friends or loved ones treated them? And how many reality shows have been produced about failing businesses run by two best friends or a husband-and-wife team whose relationships had deteriorated after becoming business partners?

These issues I've mentioned are ones you may not think about during the initial planning stages of your business but that will surface and possibly accumulate along the way. It's up to you to decide how big or small they become, and how willing you are to accept them and carry on.

Equity Deals: Consider What You're Getting vs. What You're Giving Up

One phenomenon I've seen many times is equity deals in which a start-up entrepreneur accepted free work in exchange for a stake in the business. They'd end up with say, a senior developer working for free who now owns 10 percent of the company, an unpaid graphic designer who now owns 5 percent of the company, etc. Not once have I seen one of those deals end well.

When someone has a stake in the business, no matter how small it is, they suddenly feel like they have certain entitlements. And even though giving up 5 percent might not sound like much when you're first starting out, as the company grows it can open a whole other can of worms. What if you have a falling out with one of those minority stakeholders? You might find yourself stuck in a buyout scenario. And at what valuation? Obviously that stakeholder is going to envision a larger valuation than you to maximize their buyout, and you might even end up in court.

And what if you decide to look for private funding and find an investor willing to put up money that you feel you need, but they want half the business, and you've already given away 15 percent for free work, meaning you could be left with a minority stake in your own company? Think long-term. Avoid these barter deals if you can and maintain your equity.

Podcasting: Lack of Consistency Kills

I get asked often about starting a website or a YouTube channel, so let me address that.

My website Fightful.com bled money initially because I naively believed that I could spend money on traffic, send users to the website, and they would become habitual visitors thereby establishing a userbase. I spent tens of thousands of dollars on traffic, and our numbers didn't progressively incline as I'd expected. Why? Because I'd underestimated the power of Google and social media.

According to Demand Sage, 93 percent of web experiences begin on a search engine. (Ruby 2023) And according to SparkToro, Google had over 90 percent of the U.S. search market share by 2018. (Fishkin 2018) Our website was new meaning we received no organic traffic, and because most people tend to start online with a search engine, most of the traffic we bought ended up in a black hole.

I decided to pivot, I scrapped our media buys, and I put more emphasis into our social media channels. Eventually thanks to Sean Ross Sapp's efforts with breaking news, our social media numbers grew, and our website numbers grew with them. But it took a lot of time and a lot of patience to get there.

Patience. That is one thing I would advise anyone to have who wants to launch a website or YouTube channel. Unless you already have some sort of celebrity status and existing following, it will take time for your numbers to grow.

But even more so than patience, it takes consistency.

Most YouTube channels will fail. And there are several reasons for that, including the quality of the content or too much competition. But a major reason why most channels fail is that content creators don't maintain a consistent schedule.

I think that when most people launch a new content platform, they're motivated by unrealistic expectations. They think they've got a great idea that will take off and in no time, they'll be posting pictures of their silver play button awarded by YouTube for reaching 100,000 subscribers. They become discouraged when their content doesn't put up the kinds of numbers they were expecting. From there, their consistency declines, ending all hope of growing a successful platform.

I launched KnowYourNews.com in 2022 about real, weird news stories. I did it for two reasons. For one, I originally owned the KnowYourNews domain many years ago, had the opportunity to reacquire it, and decided to for nostalgia reasons. And two, I like weird news stories.

Fightful taught me a lot about having realistic expectations, and so KnowYourNews lost money every single month and I wasn't at all surprised by it. But I kept it going for almost two years because I liked the concept. And I made sure that the content team was consistent, and so we saw some very slow growth in our YouTube and social media numbers, and the positive momentum was all the motivation I needed to carry on.

Unfortunately, as views, likes, and follows became a hot commodity in the social media world, they led to an unending supply of staged and fake content created for the sake of user engagement. And that meant that a platform with real content like KnowYourNews got lost in the shuffle because people couldn't decipher one from the other. So ultimately, I made the decision to cut my losses and move on from 'KYN'. But I don't regret doing it. I would have rather tried and failed than not tried at all.

If you want to be a podcaster or content creator, don't do it for the money. That is the biggest piece of advice that I can give to anyone who aspires to launch a content platform in this era. Patience and consistency go without saying, but don't do it for the money. Do it for the love of it.

THE STORYTELLING SALESMAN

We're proud of our YouTube Creator Award for passing 100,000 subscribers with Fightful.

7
Shenanigans: Go with Your Gut

BETRAYAL OVER MONEY CERTAINLY DOESN'T JUST HAPPEN BETWEEN business partners. It can happen with employees as well, especially in a sales environment.

In every business, when you hire an employee, you bestow on them a certain level of trust, and you take on a certain level of risk with respect to them potentially stealing information and/or cutting side deals to benefit themselves at your expense. It's a part of business and something you must be wary of, especially in the post-pandemic world where a lot of people work remotely, and it's harder to monitor their day-to-day activities. I've learned from experience to go with my gut—if something smells fishy, it probably is.

Early in the existence of my company, I hired a sales executive named Derek. I knew Derek well because I had hired and trained him at a previous place of work, and he became somewhat of a protégé of mine. I left that job to start my own business, and he left to go to a competitor. The opportunity didn't work out for him there, and he became available, and so I hired him. I knew him, I knew his work ethic, and I felt I could trust him given our previous history.

For the first six months that Derek was with us, he did a great job. He closed a lot of deals, drove a lot of revenue for us, and was very hands-on with respect to receivables and staying on top of delinquent accounts. Then he referred his friend Barry who was looking for a sales job in our area, as he was moving from out west.

Now, Barry was a charming, personable guy who said all the right things, and so based largely on Derek's recommendation, we hired him—and this was my lesson on why you shouldn't hire friends of employees. We also helped Barry find an apartment locally and paid some of his moving expenses. We hoped that we'd found another competent, motivated sales executive to help drive revenue.

As time passed, it became apparent to us that Barry and Derek's commitment to the company wasn't there.

For one, Barry wasn't closing any business at all. He told us going in that he was new to our industry and would need time to build a Rolodex, but it was unusual for someone to generate almost no revenue months into the job. Plus, Barry was heavily active in the industry Meta (Facebook) groups and seemingly everyone knew him, which further raised suspicions about his numbers.

In addition to that, Derek's performance fell off a cliff. New deals stopped coming in, his outstanding receivables began to add up, and two-hour trips to the gym in the middle of the workday became a daily routine.

We also noticed that Barry would walk home on his lunch break, saying he wanted to spend time with his wife and their dog, but his Skype would pop online as soon as he left, and that was typically how people communicated in our industry at the time. My suspicions started to grow that these two were up to something. I didn't want to believe it given my closeness to Derek, but the warning signs were too strong.

It came time for an industry conference in San Francisco, and myself, my partner Luke, Derek, and Barry all went. From the moment we got to the hotel, Derek and Barry were like ghosts. We never heard from them or saw them until the final evening of the trip when we'd planned a company dinner. And neither were talkative at that dinner, seemingly preferring to be somewhere else. We flew home believing they were working on a side business, and we'd need to act. And then the puzzle pieces fell into place.

One morning, Barry's computer wasn't working properly. I called an IT consultant to come to the office to check it out. He had to access Barry's computer to fix the problem, and while he did, Barry stood behind him the entire time nervously pacing. It seemed very clear to us that he didn't want something to be seen on that computer.

Around that time, Derek went on vacation to Europe. While he was gone, I got a phone call that lifted the curtain on the entire situation.

I was told by a long-time friend of mine in the industry that Barry was working for a competitor and essentially driving business away from us directly to them. My friend found out because one of his clients had mentioned to him in passing that they were working with that competitor and that their contact was Barry. But my friend thought that Barry worked for me and called me to inquire about it, thinking maybe we had parted ways, which we hadn't.

Upon further investigation, I discovered that that competitor was also a client of Derek's with us, and that their receivables had not been paid in months. I had a policy that I would not allow new business with any delinquent client. And so, my hunch was that Derek had intentionally neglected that account to ensure we wouldn't continue working with them and potentially uncover their ruse. We decided it was time to make a move.

My plan was to wait for Derek to return from vacation so that I could fire Barry and him at the same time. But I think that Derek got wind of the fact that we'd figured out their little operation. The day that he was scheduled to return, he called in sick. The day after that, he called and resigned over the phone, saying he didn't want to return to the office. I implored him to come in to talk to me in person, but he refused. We then proceeded to fire Barry.

A few days later, Barry asked us to join him for lunch where he told us that he'd been advised not to sign the termination paperwork we'd prepared, which didn't surprise me since it included a non-compete clause, and we knew he'd been quietly working for that competitor the whole time. He turned in quite a performance, even shedding a tear before asking us if there were any companies we didn't want him to work for because he would honor that request. I was tempted to name the company we knew he was at but chose to stay quiet.

From there, Barry posted a lengthy message in an industry Meta (Facebook) group declaring we had fired him and playing the victim. Many of the people in those groups who didn't know the real story villainized us, but we chose to stay silent realizing we'd be in a no-win situation if we reacted.

Eventually, both guys went public with their "new" place of work. They managed to pull some business away from us but nothing significant, and I went about recruiting, hiring, and training new sales staff.

The aftermath exemplified good karma. We built out a whole new team and hit record growth each year. As for Derek and Barry, eventually they both left that competitor, had a falling out, and drifted apart. Derek went on to jump from company to company for many years, while Barry seemingly disappeared from that industry.

A group photo at our annual Toronto Blue Jays company outing. Look at those smiles!

In a "coming full circle" moment, years later Derek became an independent consultant and worked with some of our clients. I was told that he wanted to bury the hatchet, and reluctantly agreed to talk to him. He apologized for his actions back then and indicated that he had matured and was now a husband and a father. I accepted his apology, but just because I forgive doesn't mean I forget. I'm not sure that a round of pints will be in our future anytime soon!

This was not the first time that I experienced an employee turning their back on their employer in the name of the almighty dollar. And living in a digital world as we do, it's amazing how sloppy if not flat-out stupid some of these people were with respect to their inability to cover their tracks.

While at Incentaclick, a couple of co-workers conspired to leave the company, go work for a competitor, and attempt to take their accounts with them. One of those people not only printed out their new employment agreement on a company printer, but they e-mailed their signed agreement to their new employer through their company e-mail!

A colleague once told me a similar story from her place of work. Two of her co-workers had started a competing business, and they had the brilliance to not only create contract and invoice templates for their own business using their work computers, but they left hard copies in their desks.

Unfortunately, the Derek saga was not an isolated incident. There have been many other times over the years at my own company that I experienced an employee doing side business under the table to benefit themselves at our expense.

One salesperson, after I found out and fired him but didn't tell him I knew what he'd been doing, offered to continue working for free since he obviously wanted to keep getting free intel for his other employer. He even told prospective clients that he was a founding partner in our business and spoke disparagingly about Luke and me.

Another person left the chat programs open on his computer after his employment had ended, revealing that he had been talking to some unscrupulous clients about leaking them information.

Yet another decided to use our company e-mail to conduct much of his side business, leaving a massive paper trail.

Money leads to shenanigans, it's human nature. The more successful you become either running your own business or leading someone else's, the more likely you'll face this problem. Keep your eyes and ears open and go with your gut.

8
Working from Home: It Ain't Always Great

AH ... WORKING OUT OF YOUR OWN HOME. WHAT A GREAT WAY TO save money if you've got a start-up business and what a great convenience if you're an employee.

On the surface, this sounds like a dream come true. You have no commute so you can sleep in longer and avoid traffic, not to mention winter conditions! But as I and many others discovered thanks to COVID, working from home isn't all it's cracked up to be. As the weeks go by, it can become difficult for an entrepreneur to stay motivated knowing that you have nowhere to go and can essentially work in your pajamas.

There's even research to back up the potential negative effects of working from home. Dan Schawbel wrote an article for Harvard Business Review about a survey he conducted in partnership with Virgin Pulse that found that while a third of the global work force always or often works remotely, two thirds aren't engaged in their job. More so than that, 100 percent of remote workers felt isolated always or very often, and nearly 60 percent felt lonely as a result. (Schawbel 2018)

Another study by UK Biobank conducted between April 2007 and December 2010 showed that those who feel isolated and lonely have an increased risk of heart attack and stroke. (Smith, et al. 2021)

Maybe this all sounds a bit too overdramatic, but there's something to be said for waking up in the morning, getting cleaned up, and heading out the door with someplace to go.

When I started my business, I at least had the benefit of living and working in a detached home, whereas my partner Luke was living and working in a small condo. But within weeks, we both felt stir-crazy and knew we needed a separate workspace. That's when I discovered the concept of a shared office.

In case you're unfamiliar, there are probably corporate buildings in your city right now that contain co-working and shared office spaces. They're basically regular offices owned or managed by a company that rents out either individual rooms in the office or individual workstations. You then share the office amenities like a front-desk secretary or a printer or kitchen. Shared spaces are much cheaper to rent than a standard office, and the terms are much more flexible, with the space being available on a month-to-month or even week-to-week basis as opposed to a multi-year lease.

Moving business operations out of our homes and into a shared office proved to be more efficient and helped us to become more engaged. Eventually, as the business started to grow, we were ready for our first full-time hires, who we brought into the shared space with us. We continued to grow and stayed in that space due to the term flexibility and cost until we simply outgrew it and had to move on.

A section of our open-concept Aware Ads office; typical for a digital company, yet efficient!

I know that the pandemic has changed our lives and remote work has become commonplace. But if you can, at least going out once a week to meet with your team in person could prove to be beneficial, even if it's at a coffee shop.

Of course, the dark side to having remote staff is that it's harder to keep tabs on their activity on a day-to-day basis.

You hear stories a lot now about remote workers taking on second or third jobs and their employers not knowing they're doing it. They'll be responsive just enough to make you think they're engaged, but then you'll notice that tasks aren't getting done in a timely fashion or they'll go silent at certain hours of the day.

Once, when an employee's productivity had gone downhill with us, they were let go and soon after posted a message on social media suggesting that if you hate your job, get yourself fired. They then posted a link to their new OnlyFans page making it clear where much of their effort had likely been devoted.

Another time, after our office reopened post-COVID, an employee said they had to continue working remotely due to family issues. Their productivity also fell off and we later discovered that they had secretly launched a competitive business during the pandemic and had shifted client accounts over and impacted our revenue, all while collecting a full-time paycheck and health benefits from us.

I've even had friends admit that their employers would have them clock in in the morning through a virtual network used to monitor staff engagement, but the employers wouldn't do much else the rest of the day aside from occasionally checking in, and so my friends would clock in via their smart phones, then take most of the day off for leisure activities and check in just enough to appease their boss if they happened to be looking for them.

A lot of trust goes into allowing someone to earn a full-time living from you while working out of their home and being very much unmanaged day-to-day. Be cognizant of your remote staff's productivity as well as the timeliness of their correspondence.

9

Know the Law: When Success is Followed by Empty Threats

THEY SAY THAT ONLY TWO THINGS IN LIFE ARE CERTAIN: DEATH AND taxes. As a business owner, paying taxes is inevitable. Of course, I could probably write another book about carry-forward losses and R&D tax credits and lots of other boring stuff. But my point here is this—get good advice. Invest in hiring a reputable accountant and a reputable attorney. Understand the law and understand your rights. The money they can help you save can offset their respective costs.

I started my company as somewhat of a virgin when it came to tax and corporate law. I knew my industry, and I knew what steps to take to make money. But I didn't know what steps I could take to save more money under the auspices and with the blessing of the federal government. And so right out of the gate, the first decision that I made was to find a corporate attorney.

I didn't need to hire someone full-time in-house (certainly didn't have the budget or enough work for that) but I got lucky—my wife introduced me to a friend of hers who was a young, aggressive corporate lawyer working for a major firm. We hit it off immediately and are close friends to this day—which is VERY important, because the more successful you become, the more you'll find yourself talking to your lawyer—and through his connections, I created a network that included corporate accountants, tax accountants, bankers, and employment lawyers. I met with them all—and have continued to regularly as the years have passed—I asked them loads of questions, and I soaked up information like a sponge.

A very common practice is for business owners to incorporate a company and register the business in the name of the company. You can then pay yourself a lesser personal salary and leave the balance of the income in the company and pay yourself a dividend with the after-tax corporate funds. If you leave after-tax corporate funds in your company and don't spend it, you don't pay additional tax on it until the funds are distributed from the company. Income earned on the after-tax corporate funds left in the company (i.e. investment income) will be taxed in the company, not by you personally.

And again depending on where your business is registered, you can move money between corporations tax-free. For example, let's say you want to buy an investment property for rental purposes. So long as it isn't your primary residence, you can create a holding company for that property, loan the funds to the holding company from your other company, and use that money tax-free to buy the property. You'll have to pay tax on the rental income and capital gains on any profits when you sell it, but the benefits are clear.

Registering your business to a company also provides a layer of security with respect to liability. If you ever found yourself in legal trouble pertaining to your company, the complainant would likely have to go after the assets of your company as opposed to your personal assets. On several occasions when a deadbeat client owed us money, and we had to take the legal route, we'd have a hard time collecting because they'd have limited assets in whatever company we'd signed a contract with. Not suggesting you create a company to do that! But I think you get my point.

Of course, laws differ depending on where your company resides. So, before you start your business, find a good corporate attorney and good accountant, and decide which options are best for you.

Once your business is up and running and your notoriety increases, the legal advice doesn't end, and if anything, the necessity for it escalates. It becomes more likely that someone may come out of the woodwork with a frivolous legal threat looking to get something out of you. But if you have access to a good corporate lawyer, ensure your business dealings involve contracts, and know your rights, you can save yourself some headaches and subsequently some money.

Early in my company's existence, I hired a young sales rep who had had a falling-out with his last employer. I reviewed his termination paperwork to ensure that we honored his contractual obligations there. After he started with us, his former employer sent us a legal letter full of frivolous accusations demanding certain monetary damages.

I knew we had done nothing wrong, so we responded basically telling them to go ahead and sue, and then they quietly went away. One of the co-founders even called me a couple of years later to apologize. It was my first small taste of the legal process, and without having the right circle of people to help me I may have mishandled the situation, but instead it resolved itself easily.

I've always been a big believer in providing added value for your clients wherever and whenever possible. My company had an in-house graphic design team, and so we would design campaign web pages for clients' products free of charge, with the sole caveat being that those designs could only be used exclusively by us.

Once we designed a page that performed very well compared to competitor designs, meaning our client was generating more sales through our design than their competitors were through their own pages. It became known in the industry that that design was ours, and that our client was doing big numbers with it. Then one day we received a "Cease and Desist" letter from one of our client's competitors, claiming we had copied one of their designs and that if we didn't take it down, they would sue us.

We absolutely did not copy their design, and we knew they were simply unhappy that our client was generating more sales than they were, so they were looking for a way to stop it. Once again, we did not roll over and abide by their demands. Instead, we had our attorney respond—using a nice letter with their corporate letterhead prominently featured—requesting to see the design we had allegedly copied as well as their proof. They never replied.

I purchased a rental property for investment purposes and hired my brother-in-law Ron as my property manager to oversee the renovation of it. He hired a contractor to do the job and would complain to me about the contractor taking shortcuts with his work, or starting on tasks that didn't yet have a permit. So Ron decided to part ways with him and hire someone else.

One day Ron called me, and in a very somber voice, said he had to forward me a letter. It was sent by a lawyer on behalf of that contractor demanding that he be paid in full for the job.

Ron had never experienced a legal threat, and I could tell he was shaken by it, but I'd learned enough about such situations by that point. I again leaned on my attorney, who countered with a demand letter of our own citing all the inefficiencies in the contractor's work that we would have to pay someone else to fix. Suffice it to say he went silent after that.

I launched a website in 2016 called Fightful.com about the world of professional wrestling and combat sports, which have been lifelong passions of mine. Within a few years, it became a top destination for wrestling news, and for a while, we had a source that got us early access to the television scripts for World Wrestling Entertainment (WWE) programming, which we put on our premium service for paid subscribers.

WWE got wind of it and probably didn't like that someone was leaking the content for their shows before they aired, and so they threatened us with legal action, demanding we remove those scripts and that we give up our source. This really rattled my Managing Editor, Sean Ross Sapp, so I took charge of it.

I again knew that we had done nothing wrong, and I also knew that we could rely on source protection, meaning we couldn't be forced to reveal a news source. So I refused WWE's demands. But I also recognized the value of a positive relationship with them, which we still have to this day.

I offered a compromise. I said that we would stop posting the actual scripts, but we would still post our own written summaries, and I would not reveal the source. They seemed fine with that, and the matter went away.

Former WWE superstar Matt Riddle wearing a Fightful T-shirt during the live weekly Fightful podcast he did with us prior to signing with WWE.

I still chuckle when I think about that time because while I was talking to WWE, a terrified Sean had started deleting the scripts from our premium service, which was essentially hurting my leverage. "Put them back! Put them back!" I pleaded.

In every one of these cases, everything worked out just fine. Knowing my legal rights, having a good attorney, and not succumbing to the pressure brought on by frivolous claims really helped me towards a positive outcome each time.

10
Juggling Good Ethics and a Good Income

SOMETIMES, AS AN EMPLOYEE, YOU HAVE TO WEIGH THE GOOD AND the bad of your job situation and balance your morals with your paycheck. And sometimes, as an employer, you have to think ahead and try to foresee any potential negative repercussions of your actions, even if your intentions are good and your actions are met with approval by seemingly everyone.

I think we've all experienced situations at our place of work at one time or another that walked the line of morals and good ethics, if not stepped right over it. Situations that made us question if it was worth staying at that job for that paycheck.

My first job out of university was at a small financial services company that provided consumer loans. They predominantly worked in the sub-prime market, meaning their typical customer had bad credit and couldn't get a loan from the big banks.

We handled customer financing for a retail furniture chain. Have you ever seen promotions on television like, "Don't pay for two years!"? Well, if you didn't pay off your living room set within those two years, you ended up in my queue, and I'd be calling you to transfer your furniture bill into a loan with us.

The interest rates were exorbitant. We're talking rates in the 30 percent to 50 percent range in many cases. It wasn't uncommon for someone to come in looking for $1,000 to pay their bills and end up owing us $1,500-plus at the end of a short-term loan.

We were also pressured by management to upsell customers on options like car insurance or roadside assistance services, because the company earned a premium on those even though we didn't get any commission. They would keep a regular tally of how many deals we were closing, which included not just loans but upsells as well. A lot of the clientele were desperate or not overly educated, and so they'd agree to whatever you offered them. Anything to get that loan.

My manager once took me out for drinks after work and told me that he was grooming me to become a manager of my own store location. He made the job sound big time. But I knew otherwise. One of his regular tasks was to drive to the homes of customers who were late on their loan payments to get a commitment on a payment or even repossess their vehicle if they'd put it down as collateral on their loan. I would hear his phone calls where irate customers would verbally abuse him. And on a couple of occasions, they even stormed into the office to berate him in person. No thanks! That was not the job for me.

Within a couple of months, I hated going to work because I felt like I was cheating these customers due to the high interest rates. But it was my first job out of school, my parents were proud, and I'd even moved into my first apartment in the town where the company was located. So I felt I had to stick it out. But my productivity suffered because I didn't like the work, and I wasn't motivated. I went from being one of the highest producers to the lowest producer within a few months. And eventually I was fired. But as much as I dreaded having to tell my parents at the time, I was so relieved that I wouldn't have to step foot in that place again.

In 1998 when I was twenty-four years old, I decided to make the move from a small country town to the big city of Toronto, Canada. I was trying to find my place in life, and I didn't feel that a small town provided me with a lot of opportunities. I quickly landed my first job, and what a job it was. I sold job-search VHS tapes to schools, libraries, or other outlets that provided resources to the unemployed.

Depending on when you were born, you probably don't even know what a VHS or "Video Home System" cassette tape is. In 1998 they were still prevalent, but I wasn't keen on the way this company went about their business. You would cold call these places, most of which had shoestring budgets at best. You would offer them a free trial of the tapes, but there was a catch: they would have to pay an exorbitant shipping and handling fee. And if they didn't return the tapes by the end of the trial period, they would be billed, and the price tag wasn't cheap—hundreds of dollars per set even though they cost very little to produce.

Some of our prospective clients were lucky if their budget was a few hundred dollars for an entire year. So I always felt uneasy with the business model. But I was new to the big city, I had rent to pay, and I needed that job, so I pushed on.

Fortunately, on the side I was working on my pro wrestling website and learning how to sell advertising. It started to take off, and so I quit this day job to focus on the site full-time. And I've always remembered my boss's comment when I gave him my notice and told him my intentions. He said I was, "going away to join the circus," and predicted it would fail and I would be back.

Once, while working at Incentaclick, I was in Las Vegas for a conference, and I treated a client to lunch who had also traveled into town for the weekend's industry events.

The business at that time was dominated by males in their twenties and thirties, and conferences were loaded with parties and alcohol and lots of other extracurricular activities.

My day-to-day client contact was a young woman, and her boss was a man in his forties. From the moment we met at the restaurant, I knew he was inebriated. Over the next couple of hours, he continued to drink and made several sexually explicit comments to his employee. I distinctly remember when she took a sip of her drink, he yelled out, "I knew it!" When she questioned what he was talking about, he said, "I knew you swallowed." She gave me a very embarrassed look, and because he was a big revenue generator for my company, I said nothing.

When lunch ended, I was planning to head back to my company's booth at the conference. My contact's boss went to the bathroom, at which point she pulled me aside and told me that she was immediately heading to the hotel to pack her bag and then going to the airport and flying home, because she had decided to quit that job. And she did.

My Weekend with the Champ

In 2013 my company experimented with launching our own workout supplement product. I had a friend in the world of credit card processing, so we partnered with him. And it just so happened that his brother-in-law Jacob had connections to former boxing champion Evander Holyfield.

I was introduced to Jacob, who told me he could get Evander to be the spokesperson for the product. And I was assured that we could get him at a very reasonable price. And so we brought Jacob in as a partner on the venture.

Jacob cut a deal that gave Evander a small percentage of sales revenue with no upfront guaranteed money. He also arranged for Evander to appear at an industry party we were sponsoring that August at a trade show in Philadelphia called the Affiliate Summit East.

We met Evander for dinner prior to the party, and he couldn't have been kinder and more gracious. He also stood out—he got recognized by everyone at the restaurant, and his reaction told me that he dealt with that all the time.

The industry party that night was called the Affiliate Ball. It took place at a nightclub, and the promoter had booked popular rapper Busta Rhymes as a feature act. I had informed the promoter in advance that we were bringing Evander to promote our product, and they advertised Evander's appearance as well.

During the party, we brought Evander from our private booth upstairs onto the main floor to take pictures with guests. That turned out to be a mistake. Not only did he get mobbed for photos, but he also got verbally abused by more than one intoxicated guest who criticized him for reportedly going broke despite earning hundreds of millions over the course of his career. (Fermie 2020) Evander just stood there silently and took the abuse before security got involved, and I felt bad for him.

The promoter of the industry party had created their own award called The AFFY, which they claimed was "in recognition of outstanding Internet achievement." That night, not only did they present an award to select industry members, but they even called Evander up on stage and presented him with one. It was clear it was done for a photo op and for attention. And that wasn't lost on Evander at all.

Sitting in a limousine heading back to Evander's hotel, I apologized to him for what he'd experienced, but he brushed it off, said not to worry, and that he had experienced worse. Then, as he exited the car, he left that AFFY award behind. I picked it up to hand it to him, and he said, "You keep it. They only gave it to me for showing up." He knew it.

The AFFY Award given to Evander Holyfield that he
left in the car and told me to keep (and I did).

Jacob had arranged for Evander to join us for lunch the next day, along with select clients that we had invited. It was a great time, and Evander was more than happy to answer questions and tell stories from his career. But then came a moment that I regret witnessing.

After that lunch ended and the clients left, Evander sat at a table while Jacob put various papers in front of him and told him to sign them. I don't know what those papers were for, and it's possible that one of them pertained to our product line. But without reading them, Evander obliged and signed. It felt to me like he was being taken advantage of.

Our product line never took off, and we quietly discontinued it. We discovered that while my age group revered a former world class athlete like Evander Holyfield, the younger male demographic that we were targeting unfortunately did not. But I'll always remember that weekend in Philadelphia because of how cool Evander was to me, and because of the way I saw him get treated by his supposed management and his supposed fans.

Me standing next to the former World Heavyweight Champion after dinner in Philadelphia.

The industry I was involved in for many years, including with AZ Ads, with Incentaclick, and with my own company was affiliate marketing, also known as performance marketing.

When I first got into the business, on the surface it sounded great. Advertisers, i.e., the owner(s) of the product or service you're marketing, wouldn't have to pay for website views or clicks on a banner ad; they'd only have to pay for results, meaning leads or sales depending on what the advertiser was looking for. You would then utilize your network of affiliates, i.e., traffic suppliers, to generate Internet traffic and send prospective customers to the advertiser's product page. You would get paid a commission for every lead or sale your affiliate generated for that advertiser, and a percentage of that commission would in turn be paid to the affiliate.

I loved the business model. Your clients would only have to pay for results. It sounded like a win-win for everybody. Well, not so much.

The problem was most affiliates only cared about their own profitability. It didn't matter to them if we were hurt financially by their actions or if our advertiser was. They would intentionally buy traffic in the wrong demographic if it was cheaper, or make false claims about the product's performance, or use celebrity likenesses without permission; anything to maximize their profits.

And they were good at hiding their identities online, meaning if a customer had a complaint, they would bypass the affiliate and go straight to the advertiser, who often was in the dark with respect to an affiliate's marketing practices.

It wasn't uncommon for an affiliate's ads to result in a consumer seeing a charge on their credit card that exceeded the amount they thought they were paying. The consumer would then call their credit card company to have their purchase refunded, causing high chargebacks for the advertiser. And the banks would in turn charge the advertiser exorbitant fees if their chargebacks exceeded a certain threshold.

We would sometimes have to cut deals with advertisers on their bills due to high chargebacks, or we'd risk them trying to skip out on the whole thing. And if we held payment from an offending affiliate, they would threaten to attempt to damage our reputation by posting in all the industry social media groups that we didn't pay our bills and to not work with us.

We also encountered some dishonest advertisers who wouldn't pay their invoices and would try to dodge us and go silent. If we were able to get to them through legal means, they would often point the finger at fraudulent affiliate traffic as an easy out even though that wasn't always the case.

I grew to dislike and distrust much of the clientele in that space, and for many years I was tolerant, because our company did well financially and provided a good quality of life for myself and my family. But eventually it became one of the reasons why I chose to leave the business. I'd reached the point where the money wasn't enough any longer.

Sometimes, even if your intentions are good, be cognizant of how they could be viewed by others, or how they could be used by others to benefit themselves at your expense.

One thing that we used to do at my company with good intentions and as a team-building exercise sort of came back to bite us. I don't consider this to be bad ethics at all; in fact, I always considered it a good and positive experience. But I'm mentioning it because of the repercussions we dealt with later.

Years before we got into business together, Luke and I would do food challenges with our friends. I don't remember how and when they started, but whenever we'd be at a restaurant, and we'd see a huge-volume item on the menu, we'd challenge a friend to eat it all for cash.

Once we were at a sports bar, and they had their own promotion: whoever could eat their big meal—which included pounds of steak, French fries, coleslaw, etc.—within a specified time, would get the meal for free and get their name on a plaque on the wall. Luke and I threw in an extra thousand dollars to entice a friend to do it. He was unsuccessful, but it made for a fun time as everyone, even complete strangers, gathered around to watch and cheer him on.

So, after we launched our company, we sometimes offered food challenges to employees.

It started on a whim. We happened to be at a grocery store, walked by the coolers, and I pointed to the sticks of butter and asked an employee how many of those he would eat for $1,000. I can't recall how many sticks we agreed to, but he excitedly accepted the challenge thinking it would be easy, but discovered it wasn't and didn't finish.

Over time the challenges evolved and became a tradition at company parties. Sort of like the game show "Let's Make a Deal," we would have gift boxes with an undisclosed amount of cash in each one. We would take volunteers for a food challenge such as, whoever could eat a Caesar salad the fastest. When someone won a challenge, they'd pick a box. At the end of the night, they would choose to either open their box and keep the contents or trade it for another box and open that one. Sometimes it would work out better for them, and sometimes it wouldn't.

Our staff were always enthusiastic about the food challenges, and there was never a shortage of volunteers. It became a positive team-building event full of camaraderie.

It was common for new hires to tell me prior to a company event that they'd heard about the food challenges and couldn't wait. On a few occasions, I even had wait staff at the venue ask if they could participate. And on one humorous occasion, all the chefs came out of the kitchen and lined up against a wall to watch. People would take pictures and videos on their phones, and it'd be the talk of the office the following week.

So, here's my point—we had an employee start a competing business with a former employee during the pandemic, and the situation was serious enough that we chose to take legal action. In an attempt to get the case dismissed, their legal team tried to paint us as bad guys, and one thing they tried to use in their efforts was the food challenges. They tried to spin it as a negative activity, suggesting we forced people to participate, and it created a bad work environment, none of which was true. Meanwhile we had photos and videos of both individuals having a great time at such events, voluntarily participating in the challenges, and one of them even hugged me after he won.

Card is Subject to Change

In early 1999 while operating my website full-time, I found out that a pro wrestling company based in Minnesota called the AWA Superstars of Wrestling was looking for someone to design and manage their web presence.

My dream back then was to work full-time in the wrestling business in a creative capacity, and I felt that this would be a great first step. I reached out to the owner, listed as Dale R. Gagne in a press release, and subsequently landed a part-time job that would allow me to continue operating my own site.

Gagne claimed to be a distant relative of wrestling legend and original American Wrestling Association (AWA) promoter, Verne Gagne, but I eventually discovered that his real name was Dale Gagner and so I doubt the validity of that claim.

Most, if not all, of Gagner's wrestling events were produced at American casino hotels and state fairgrounds where local officials would pay him a lump sum to draw in prospective customers, so

Gagner knew his profits up front and wouldn't have to rely on ticket sales to make money. These types of events are known in that business as sold shows.

Gagner flew me in for one such event at the Red River Valley Fair in Fargo, North Dakota, in June of 1999, where I got to rub elbows with some of the legends I'd grown up watching, including WWE Hall of Famers such as The Bushwhackers, the late George "The Animal" Steele, The Iron Sheik, and the late "Sensational" Sherri Martel. I also got to meet up-and-comers in the business, such as current WWE on-air personality Adam Pearce and current All Elite Wrestling (AEW) ring announcer Justin Roberts. It was a great time that made me excited about a potential future in that industry.

A young goateed me with WWE Hall of Famers "Sensational" Sherri Martel (left) and Butch and Luke of the Bushwhackers (right).

Wrestling once had the reputation of being a low-brow form of entertainment run by unethical promoters known for over-hyping yet under-delivering on events, not to mention short-changing their talent roster on money. Gagner was somewhat of a throwback to that time, because eventually his actions made me question his legitimacy.

Gagner would regularly send me pictures and other materials to use on the website, and one day, he sent me a caricature of Jesse Ventura, who was a former AWA wrestler, and who had become the popular Governor of the state of Minnesota. The picture included a dialogue bubble, like what you'd see in a comic book, coming out of Ventura's mouth that said, "AWA Wrestling is GREAT!" along with the caption "The GOV Sez" under Ventura's picture. I was asked to feature that on the main page of the website, and I could see how people might be misled to believe that Ventura was affiliated with the company, which was not the case.

In February of 2000, the AWA held an event at the Riverside Casino in Laughlin, Nevada. What was most notable about that show was the absence of a star attraction who they had advertised locally, but who didn't appear—former WWE Champion Mankind, also known as Mick Foley. Gagner had never mentioned Foley's name to me, and so his name never appeared on our website. It felt like a piece of false advertising designed to draw a crowd to the casino. Justin Roberts told me later that he had the difficult task of informing the crowd—most of whom were there to see Mankind—that he wouldn't be appearing, and a riot nearly ensued as a result.

That July, the AWA had an event scheduled at the Greeley Independence Stampede in Greeley, Colorado. The town's official website featured the photos of renowned wrestling stars from WWE as well as another popular national wrestling company at the time called World Championship Wrestling (WCW). Much like with Mankind previously, Gagner had not told me those names were booked, and so they weren't mentioned on the AWA website. I e-mailed the promoter in Greeley to let him know about the mistake and didn't get a response. I also asked Gagner about it, and he claimed it was a misunderstanding, and he would talk to the local promoter in Greeley.

A month later, in August of 2000, I drove to a show in St. Ignace, Michigan, along with some wrestlers from the Canadian independent scene who I had befriended and got booked on the AWA show. I was surprised to see the name "The Ultimate Warrior" advertised on an event poster at the venue under a picture of an independent wrestler known as The Luminous Warrior. The Ultimate Warrior was an enormously popular WWE star who had since retired, and, while The Luminous Warrior looked somewhat like his famous counterpart, he was certainly not the WWE legend as the poster made him out to be.

The portion of the AWA event poster that featured a picture of independent wrestler The Luminous Warrior, falsely advertised as wrestling legend The Ultimate Warrior.

I started to feel uneasy given all these issues. I loved the idea of working in the wrestling business, but I didn't love the idea of working with Dale Gagner. Then as time passed, my monthly payments stopped coming. I had agreed to a modest $500 per month for part-time work, and Gagner initially sent me checks on time like clockwork. But then they started coming late, and then they stopped coming altogether. Gagner blamed the Pitney Bowes postage meter used at his office, claiming that a lot of mail sent with the metered postage never arrived at its destination.

By October of 2000, I was owed nearly $5,000 in unpaid invoices, so I told Gagner I was suspending my work until he caught up on payment. Within a day, he blocked my e-mail account so that I couldn't e-mail him, plus he had his secretary inform me that my latest invoice (for September) would not be paid. My access to the AWA website was cut off as well. The quickness of these actions indicated to me that Gagner was expecting me to quit and had prepared for my decision.

Gagner also told me that he would be sending me a certified letter approved by his attorney and accused me of treacherous interference with his clients by sending an e-mail to the promoter in Greeley. He claimed I was responsible for financial damages. So I hired a Minnesota-based attorney and filed a complaint. We were informed that Gagner was no longer associated or working with AWA Superstars of Wrestling and my attorney suspected that there were other creditors going after Gagner's company, and so he likely walked away from it.

I never received that money. I also never received that supposed certified letter. And interestingly enough, I had spoken to a certain wrestling legend who correctly predicted that there would be no letter because I had done nothing wrong.

Feeling cheated by Gagner, I sent an e-mail to the Ultimate Warrior himself to let him know that his name had been falsely advertised at that show in Michigan. We corresponded back and forth for a little while and not only was he right about the letter, but he gave me some good advice. He suggested that I develop a better pay policy to prevent such a situation from arising again. "When it comes to these types of individuals, there is no end to the schemes they have to avoid paying the talent," he said. "Get your money up front."

WWE also went after Gagner in 2007 for trademark infringement because they owned the AWA intellectual property. (Reichel 2007) They settled the following year, and Gagner subsequently ran events under the banner "Wrestling Superstars Live". (Johnson 2008)

I don't know what became of The Ultimate Warrior's dispute with Gagner's AWA or if he ever pushed forward legally. Years later, on April 5, 2014, he was inducted into the WWE Hall of Fame. Sadly, just three days after that on April 8, Warrior passed away at the age of fifty-four from a heart attack. He had just returned home to Scottsdale, Arizona, following WWE's WrestleMania and Hall of Fame weekend in New Orleans, Louisiana, where he was a feature attraction one last time.

11
Banks: You Hate Them But You Need Them

BANKS. THEY'RE A NECESSARY EVIL. FEES, FEES, AND MORE FEES. But it's hard to get business done without them. Here are a few tips to help the process go as seamlessly as possible.

A good gauge to see which bank will be the best fit for you is to have a representative from each one in your area meet with you. Get a sense for who seems to be the most accommodating and is the best and fastest at correspondence. As you grow, you'll want to work with a bank in which your rep is reachable by phone or e-mail whenever anything comes up. And as someone who has dealt with a lot of bank employees who take days to respond to an e-mail and sometimes don't respond at all, I know how important efficient communication is.

Also, understand that the banks are very competitive and will try to one-up each other on rates and fees. I've never had a bank *not* match or beat another bank's quote on bank fees. Don't sign up with the first bank you see; shop around and compare.

You should also have each bank do a demonstration of their online interface so you can get a feel for how user friendly it is. You'd be surprised how outdated some of the banks' online platforms are. We once had a bank present their corporate wire platform to us, only to discover that it was only compatible in an outdated version of one web browser! Switching banks can be a tedious, time-sucking task once your business is running, so be confident in your choice before you make it.

Ultimately, I didn't select my bank because their fees were the lowest. I chose them because they were the most accommodating, they were the fastest with respect to correspondence, and their platform wasn't outdated, plus their fees weren't ludicrous in comparison to the others either.

Sometimes, even if you choose to work with a bank that is an internationally recognized and seemingly reputable institution, you can run into some unexpected issues if you don't do proper due diligence.

A few years into our company's existence, we wanted to expand internationally and found that we were having a tough time attracting European clients. We decided to create a European subsidiary, feeling that if it appeared that we had a presence there, it might help us to attract those vendors. That required us to work with an international bank, and we ultimately chose HSBC because they could accommodate all our needs, plus there was a local branch not far from our office.

At first, everything was great. We had not just a local bank representative, but also European reps, and we even traveled to the UK to meet them. Our local rep was excellent at correspondence and always available. But then suddenly in late 2014, she started to change.

I remember the year because on one occasion I was holding my crying newborn daughter in one arm while holding my phone with the other talking to this suddenly persistent bank rep. She would call wanting details on various international vendors and would ask question after question, which was something we'd never experienced with our local banks. And e-mails we'd send her pertaining to day-to-day operations started to go unanswered. We felt we'd need to switch banks, which would be a hassle when our subsidiary was in full swing and had credit cards and everything already set up.

Then one day, we got a letter in the mail from HSBC informing us that they were closing our accounts. We were dumbfounded! *They were firing us?!?* It didn't make any sense–until suddenly it did.

I stumbled upon a news story about HSBC admitting to money laundering for drug cartels in Mexico (Fontevecchia 2012). As I did more digging, I read a press release from the US Department of Justice from 2012 that stated that HSBC had admitted to anti-money laundering and sanctions violations by illegally conducting transactions on behalf of countries that were subject to such sanctions, including Cuba, Iran, Libya, Sudan, and Myanmar (formerly Burma) (Affairs 2012). In fact, in 2018 Netflix released an episode of their documentary series *Dirty Money* all about HSBC's ties to Mexican cartels.

Now we understood. Because the Internet is worldwide, we had clients everywhere and had wire transactions coming in and out of our account from various countries on a regular basis. I suspect that because HSBC had gotten into so much trouble, and because our homebase was Canada despite having a variety of international partners, that put us on HSBC's hypersensitive radar.

In retrospect, I guess I should have researched HSBC before we signed on with them, but they were huge, so I thought they were a safe bet. I never would have predicted the stories that we discovered later.

It's one thing to open bank accounts, it's another thing to manage them efficiently.

No matter how big my company got and how busy I was, I always ensured that my partner and I had the ultimate control of the bank accounts. Wires could be submitted by my accounting team, but they could not be approved without my or my partner's authority. E-transfers could only be done with my authority. I limited how many people in each division of the company had credit cards, monitored their statements along with my Controller, and on more than one occasion, I took someone's card away after discovering that personal expenses were being put through.

The payroll was no different. All staff members who submitted expense reports had to get sign-off from me before they'd be put into payroll. I wouldn't approve them if there was no itemized receipt—because the government may not accept it—and I also wouldn't approve expenses over $100 in which the employee hadn't given their direct manager a head's up first. It's your money. And so, it's up to you to know what goes in and what goes out.

I once had a meeting with a colleague who had worked for a competitor, and he asked me, "What kind of credit line do you have with your bank against your receivables?" That, as it turned out, was standard practice with that competitor. My answer? "I don't." The bank of course wants to maximize the fees they earn from you and will offer you a variety of tempting products with that in mind, including loans and credit lines.

I was always cognizant of keeping the company debt-free if I could. On the surface, it sounds great to take a credit line against your receivables, take the money out personally in the form of a dividend, and leave the debt in the company. But what happens if some of those receivables end up uncollectible, thereby hampering your cash flow? What happens if there's an unexpected downturn in your business, even temporarily, that makes those debt repayments a burden on your resources? What happens if you have an opportunity to get private funding, only for your investor to discover that you have bank debt, knowing that if business takes a turn for the worst, the government and the bank always get paid first?

For me, avoiding bank loans and credit lines was a good exercise on how to run an efficient, cash flow positive business. Our bank numbers were never artificial or inflated, and our profits never disappeared by way of monthly debt repayments.

And by the way, about that competitor that got a credit line against receivables—they went out of business.

12
Keep It Lean

IF YOU'RE AMONG THE SMALL PERCENTAGE OF START-UP COMPANIES that can secure millions in venture capital funding and need to scale quickly, you can probably afford to go on a mass hiring spree and fill potentially dozens of seats in a matter of months. But if your company is like most new businesses and has limited starting capital, keeping your company lean is crucial to your longevity.

You might be surprised to discover that a lot of people who are open to new employment opportunities enjoy a start-up environment and understand the expectation to "wear multiple hats." Some of these people might come from the corporate world, are tired of that buttoned-up corporate culture, and long for a more laid back, more relaxed environment that typically comes with a young company.

Others might find it appealing to be able to take on a job with a variety of responsibilities that will allow them to learn different skills and will ensure that their days aren't repetitive and tedious.

Look to fill positions with "hybrid" roles whenever possible when you're starting out. If for example, you need a graphic designer, but you don't think that you have forty hours of work per week available for them, maybe they can take on other tasks that complement that role, such as front-end development work, or copywriting, or internal media buying to ensure that their job is truly full-time and that they're paying for their seat, so to speak.

There's always the option to hire someone on a part-time hourly contract, and for your business maybe that's the right solution. From my experience, it was more difficult for those people to become integrated with the rest of the team, and so my preference was always to find enough work to warrant hiring someone full-time.

Now, don't allow your workforce to be *too* lean; know when it's time to fill a seat. A proper work-life balance is also important. And wearing multiple hats might be a necessary reality at first when starting a business, but it can also cause you to feel burned out. Plus, spreading yourself too thin can slow your company's momentum.

For example, if you can only devote an hour a day to social media work when your company could use three or four hours, what are you losing by being so hands-on and keeping your employee head count too low?

On several occasions, I would take on a task that I just didn't have the time to do efficiently, and the work would suffer as a result. I knew I needed help, but that didn't necessarily mean I had to add to our payroll. I would look at my team, their workload, their respective skillsets, and if applicable, I would offer someone the opportunity to scale back on their current tasks just enough to devote time to this new one.

Every time, the employee seemed to appreciate the new opportunity, not to mention the chance to learn and do something different. And every time, the result turned out better than if the job had stayed on my plate with not enough time to devote to it. And if my team's time was maxed out, and they couldn't realistically take on more work without impacting their current tasks, *then* I would look at a new hire.

Even as your business grows and you continue to hire new staff, it's important to ensure that there is a need for a full-time, forty-hours-per-week person before you recruit.

I would often take a stroll around the office and glance at monitors to see how many people were on YouTube or social media to give me an idea of how busy they were in case their manager came to me looking to add to the team.

For years, it was very common in my business for my competitors doing similar revenue numbers as us if not less, to have anywhere from two times to as many as ten times the staff in their office. They would have Directors reporting to Directors reporting to Directors. It was clear that a lot of their profits were being eaten up by overhead and inevitable that they would be forced to downsize, which would in turn damage their reputation both externally as well as internally.

One explanation I heard a lot was, "They're looking to sell and so they went on a hiring spree to make the company growth look impressive to a potential buyer." I had investors approach me on a few occasions and never was their first question, "How many people do you have?" Top line revenue, gross profit, net income—the financial numbers are what matter most.

Don't fall into the trap of hiring people you don't need because you think that's what's supposed to happen when you grow. Hire as needed.

The Cheapest Option is Not Necessarily the Best Option

A temptation you might encounter, especially if you're on a tight budget and/or don't have enough work to justify a full-time person, might be to hire someone freelance on a remote basis. Key thing to remember here is this: you get what you pay for.

When I was starting my company, I needed web development work done but not enough to warrant a full-time hire, and so I outsourced to a company out of India; their pricing was much cheaper than hiring someone locally, and so they fit my limited budget. I learned quickly why they were so modestly priced.

For one thing, they were incredibly slow both in correspondence and in hitting deadlines. And once I grew tired of the inefficiencies and replaced them with someone locally, we discovered that they had embedded code into our sites that would send copies of incoming inquiries and correspondence directly to their own servers, meaning they were basically stealing our lead data.

On another occasion, I reluctantly agreed to outsource a project to an Indian company because one of my employees had worked with them in the past and vouched for them. I was against it after my previous experience, but my employee was adamant that they did great work. Unfortunately, it was more of the same—slow correspondence and missed deadlines. And when we informed them of our decision to move the work in-house, they changed the passwords on our servers and tried to lock us out of our own platform!

Now don't get me wrong, I'm sure that there are some cost-effective international outsourced solutions that are excellent, so I'm not suggesting that you'll run into pitfalls every time, and I'm certainly not trying to brand them all as being fraudulent. But never allow your decision to come down to price.

And this isn't just about service solutions. There have historically been too many examples of companies outsourcing product manufacturing to China without proper due diligence because of the per-unit cost or substituting long-standing ingredients in a food product with a cheaper, lower quality alternative, all for the sake of improving profit margins, but the result is dissatisfied customers, lower sales, lower profits, and a downward spiral from there.

13

The Coach Doesn't Congregate with the Players

NOT ONLY IS IT COMMON FOR PEOPLE TO CHOOSE FRIENDS OR LOVED ones as business partners when starting up a business, but it's equally common for people to choose those close to them to work as employees. And I'm sure there are plenty of examples to back up that decision as a good and successful one. But from my experience, there's a reason for the saying, "Don't mix business with pleasure."

Once my company grew to the point that we were ready for our first full-time hires, we went the friend route. We did so because we'd worked with them in the past, so they knew our industry, and we trusted them. We also did so because it meant we wouldn't have to spend a bunch of time on recruitment, and interviews, and training, which were tasks we were happy to avoid given how valuable our time was, especially in those early days. In just a few short months, we learned what a mistake that was.

First and foremost, a friend isn't likely to show you the same level of respect as the boss that others in the company will. They're likely to treat you differently and take the tasks you assign them less seriously.

It's understandable if you think about it. If they're accustomed to hanging out with you on a personal level, enjoying drinks at the bar, and looking at you as a friend or colleague, it's hard for them to suddenly look at you as their boss.

You are also likely to run into entitlement issues. We frequently ran into problems with these people showing up late, or leaving early, or calling in sick when it was convenient, or taking two-hour lunch breaks, or spending hours a day on social media. It was always a problem with employees who started out as friends.

Cora was my Account Manager at a previous place of work before I brought her in to work for me at my company. She helped set up and maintain all my client campaigns.

At our old jobs, they didn't give Account Managers bonuses, and so when I had good commission months, I would give Cora cash bonuses out of my own pocket, as much as $5,000 some months. She didn't ask for it; I did it because I felt she deserved it. She worked hard, she worked after hours when needed; she even worked on Christmas Day one year when a client's server shut down, and we had to scramble to move every campaign in our system over to new web links. She was loyal, she was dedicated, and I felt she would be a valuable addition to my own team.

When Cora started with us, she had the goal of making a $60,000 annual base salary. This was a hybrid role, commissioned sales plus account management. At that time, we weren't paying anyone in a commissioned position that high a base salary. She had never earned commission and didn't realize the potential, and so she was adamant she wanted that base. So I presented her with two offers: $50,000 salary with our regular commission plan, or $60,000 salary with a reduced commission plan. I told her to pick one, and she chose the latter to get the base she wanted.

In less than two years, Cora was making double her income target between salary and commission. And yet on a regular basis, I would get attitude from her, I'd run into issues with her hours, and she would vent to other employees about how we were supposedly short-changing her on money because her commission plan was lower than other salespeople in the company. I would remind her that she was given two options, and she chose the one she chose. We ended up parting ways, mutually but not on the greatest of terms.

I also discovered after the fact that Cora had been helping Derek, another former friend and employee, by doing account management work for the competitor Derek was working with on the side while on my payroll. I wasn't surprised, although I did feel betrayed by her just as I felt betrayed by Derek after years of being not just co-workers but friends. Cora eventually reached out to apologize and wanted to reconnect. I accepted her apology but decided not to rekindle that friendship and haven't seen her since.

Not only should you be careful with respect to hiring friends, but you also need foresight when it comes to hiring employees' friends.

When I worked at Incentaclick, management would regularly accept referrals from employees for their friends. In my opinion, the owners did so quite frankly not because they didn't have the time to recruit and interview new people, but because they were simply too lazy to take that kind of initiative. Hiring friends of employees made the recruitment process easier. In time, the company had amassed a sales team comprised mostly of people who got the job by being a friend of someone else on the team.

One day we heard about a new competitor starting up with a management group that was known to be friends with a group of friends in our office. Then as the months passed, one by one, the production from those people in our office decreased. And then, one by one, they resigned. They would go off the grid long enough to fulfill the non-compete clause in their employment agreement, and then they would unsurprisingly show up as new employees for that competitor. It ruffled the feathers of our CEO and I'm sure he had sleepless nights over it. But it was a domino effect that began with the decision-making with respect to staff hires.

After my experience hiring friends when my company was in start-up mode, I never made that mistake again. I had friends inquire about work on a few occasions, and many times an employee would come to me saying they had a friend interested in an open position. Never did I go in that direction again.

I also never allowed myself to get too friendly with employees to avoid issues with entitlement or a lack of respect for my authority. I would even make a point of not joining employees for drinks after work when invited, or for lunches, or for any extracurricular outings unless it was a unique situation or a company event. I drew a line in the sand so to speak and wouldn't cross it.

Choosing candidates who were new to the industry and whom I didn't have a previous friendship with provided the most employee longevity in my experience. Not to mention, they were always less expensive, and created less stress because I wouldn't run into the same entitlement issues or lack of motivation that I would with friends or seasoned staffers.

Of course, with certain positions, experience is required. I mean if you're looking for a developer who knows Scala programming language, you're unlikely to find someone off the street new to the workforce with that experience. But with any kind of entry-level position, it's more about finding the right person with the right personality than someone with related experience on their résumé.

A couple of years into my company's existence, I wanted to diversify and create multiple revenue streams, and so we launched new business ventures under new divisions and recruited management level people to head them up.

When it came time to fill out each team with salespeople and entry-level workers, the first gut instinct of those managers every time was to look to their previous places of work and hire people they knew. Again, they figured the recruits would come with active portfolios and an understanding of the business and could get up to speed faster.

Because these were new ventures, and I wasn't as familiar with them as I was my core business, I gave those managers the freedom to recruit who they wanted. I also spent a lot of money on lawyers looking at these candidates' existing employment contracts to ensure that we honored the terms and conditions of their existing deals.

The result not only solidified what I'd learned in the past when hiring friends but magnified it.

I found that many of these hires came in with certain entitlements and expectations but also with bad habits through improper training with their previous employer. They wanted big salaries, extra vacation time, benefits starting day one, and free rein to travel to conferences around the world, all on the company dime, of course.

And what was the result? In almost every case, we would end up parting ways with these experienced people inside of a year. They had become too comfortable; they didn't have the drive or the hunger that they once did and thought they could get by based on their past successes.

But I'm a numbers guy. The bottom line is all that matters. And so, when months would go by with promises of big deals that never came to fruition and sales numbers equal to or less than what a typical new employee would generate with a fraction of the salary, it made for easy decisions.

Now let's talk about the importance of education in the job market.

To some employers, it's a big deal what school a candidate graduated from, or what their grade point average was. But for me, the educational details were never my primary interest when looking at a résumé. I did like to see that a candidate had at least graduated college, because it showed me a level of commitment and work ethic. But aside from that, I was far more interested in a person's drive and personality than I was their degree or diploma.

When you're looking to fill technical positions, it's obviously important that they come in with the proper schooling and training. But when it comes to more entry-level roles—sales, account management, and clerical type work—I've never cared that much about seeing decorated post-secondary educational credentials on a résumé.

Granted, these days it seems that everybody goes to school, and a bachelor's degree is the bare minimum that most attain, and that's fine. But nobody will ever impress me simply by boasting about their grades.

Hustle and common sense. Those are the two qualities I always looked for in a new candidate, especially in sales. They're not as easy to find as you might think, but sometimes you just have to know where to look.

Have you ever been to a sporting event and seen a salesperson sitting at a folding table pitching people to open a bank account?

Or have you ever stood in line at a coffee shop or simply walked down the street and had someone approach you about signing up for a credit card?

Companies are contracted to handle that type of "field sales" work and typically go after kids fresh out of school or new immigrants because they know they'll work cheap. And those types of jobs are a real hustle. You're talking hours spent on your feet for a minimal wage with prospective customers mostly turning you down and sometimes being rude about it.

As I learned about these types of companies and saw kids in action peddling products unsolicited, I thought, if they're good at this, they could kill it in a more professional online sales environment. So, I started recruiting for my entry-level sales positions among these street hustlers who were working for those types of companies.

What I found were young graduates, many of whom were well spoken and had confidence, but they just hadn't found the right opportunity. They would show up to work on time every day, they would put in the hours, they would hustle, and several of them stayed with me for many years.

Then there are the door-to-door B2B (business to business) salespeople. These are the folks hired to visit businesses, again unsolicited, to peddle office related products, whether printers, or paper, or coffee machines. This work also requires salespeople to be well spoken and confident to succeed, and it requires you to be good at taking rejection, but the financial rewards are often minimal.

One day I was out of the office when I got a text message from my business partner telling me about a kid who had come in to pitch office products. He said this kid was funny, he was personable, he was smart, and well spoken; he'd be a good sales candidate. But the only information he had was his first name. So I called the company's office and left a message for a person with that name, claiming we were interested in purchasing a computer printer. When he called back, I told him I didn't really want the printer, but I'd heard about his pitch, and I wanted to meet him about a potential job. He came in for a meeting, accepted a position, and became one of our longest tenured and highest producing employees.

As is common in a lot of offices, I would tend to frequent the same restaurants for lunch most days and got to know a lot of the wait staff on a first-name basis. One girl was really on the ball. She would have our drinks ready on our table before we even sat down, and she would remember every detail of our food order no matter how complicated it might be. I came to learn that she had emigrated from Europe, had a desire to work in a marketing related field, but worked at the restaurant because she didn't have a formal post-secondary education, and so interviews were hard to come by.

Time went by, and we'd see her every week, and then suddenly she was gone. Then one day, months later, she reached out to me online and told me that she'd gone home because her mother passed away, but now she had returned, was struggling to find a job, and asked if I might be able to help with referrals. She knew nothing about my industry or even general online marketing, but I knew she was competent, organized, and hardworking. Plus, she was a nice, positive person, and so I gave her a chance on a part-time contract, and it eventually blossomed into a full-time, successful Office Manager role for her that she maintained with us for many years.

Sometimes, you come across a new hire even when you're not necessarily looking.

One night I went to the movies with my wife at a theater in Toronto. As we approached the entrance to our movie, a young waiter stood out front and confidently said, "Ladies and gentlemen, welcome to the VIP!"

I proceeded to ask him where the 3D glasses were for this film and without skipping a beat he smiled and said, "Sir, your glasses are waiting for you at your seat as they should be, because you, are a VIP."

Then as we sat down, he handed us the food menu, pointed at a couple of items, and jokingly whispered, "I wouldn't get that one, that one's not good," and, "that one there, you might want to avoid that one too." He left to get our drink order and I said to my wife, "I'm going to hire this kid."

At the opportune moment I told him who I was and what I did, and that I was recruiting for a sales position and thought he had the tools to be successful in that environment. I asked him if he was still in school, and he said he'd recently graduated. I then wrote my e-mail address on a piece of paper and asked him to reach out to me if he was interested in a sales opportunity. Two weeks later he e-mailed me and admitted he'd found it odd to be pitched for a job in that setting, but he'd looked me up and wanted to talk. I brought him in for an interview and ended up hiring him full-time.

Whether you're the owner of a company or an employee who manages people, you never know where you might stumble upon a talented person who would be a great fit on your team.

Think long-term with your hires. Don't think about, will I get six months with this person, or a year? Think about, will I get five years with this person, or ten years? Surrounding yourself with people who knew you on a personal level before they knew you as their employer will get you short-term results and long-term headaches.

And always remember—your employees are there to make a living, not for a social life. You can be friendly with them, of course, but don't blur the lines between "friendly with an employee" and "friends with an employee." Because once your staff view you as a friend, that's when you'll start running into issues like what I've described.

Bringing the Recruitment Process In-House

I decided to play the long game and hire "newbies" (i.e., newcomers to our industry) as opposed to going the short and easy route and recruiting friends and/or people with experience in our business.

Along the way, I inadvertently learned a lot about recruitment.

At first, I used job-posting websites but found that I'd receive literally dozens of applications a day, mostly from people who didn't fit the work background or the candidate profile I was looking for, and, in many cases, didn't reside in the country and were looking to get sponsored to come in.

Then I turned to a recruitment agency. These types of companies will generally charge you a fee anywhere from 18 percent to 30 percent of a recruit's annual salary so long as they stay employed with you for at least three months. That means that if you hired someone for $50,000 a year, you're paying an agency anywhere from $9,000 to $15,000 as their fee.

These agencies will typically meet an applicant first and vet them, but it's still a rich fee to pay, especially when you're a small company with a small budget.

My hiring process changed when I started asking these recruits how they'd gotten in touch with the agency. Almost every time, the answer was the same: LinkedIn. It seems like everyone creates a profile there once they enter the work force.

I did some research and found that LinkedIn has a platform called LinkedIn Recruiter. It's not cheap, costing thousands of dollars a year depending on your options. But it lets you do searches and filtering by everything from keywords to location to job title to even company, industry, and graduating year, plus it enables an employer to contact prospective employees whether they're part of your LinkedIn network or not.

I figured if I hired one person a year, the service would pay for itself compared to using an agency. From then on, I did my own recruiting using LinkedIn Recruiter, found people who stayed with me for years, and saved tens of thousands of dollars in recruitment fees annually.

———■———

14

Interviews: Seeing Through the Bullshit

IF YOU'RE A MANAGER OR BUSINESS OWNER, OF COURSE YOU WON'T find the perfect fit for every job by just walking down the street and bumping into people. You will undoubtedly need to turn to recruitment options whether it be an agency, LinkedIn, or a job-search website. The trick isn't to get applications, since that part is easy. The trick is to weed through those applications effectively, identify obvious issues, and avoid any bad hires through the interview process.

For me, someone's educational background has never been the make-or-break detail to any résumé for any position. Sometimes applicants highlight their GPA, but to me it just doesn't matter.

Not to get sidetracked, but I've never been a fan of our educational system, especially at the university level. I've always believed that those who get good grades are not necessarily smarter than those who don't, they just happen to be better at memorizing information and regurgitating it out on a test.

Myself, I was always an average student at best. My classes never really interested me, and I never really gave it my all on tests or assignments. I knew that I needed to get my degree to get my foot in the door of an employer, but I didn't see a big difference between graduating with grades in the sixties or in the nineties unless I aspired to further my education in law school or medical school, which I didn't. And now, many business owners that I know were also average students, and some were even drop-outs, while many of those "top of their class" students ended up working for people like us.

The main thing I've always looked for with respect to résumés are signs of a bad hire including the following:
- Spelling mistakes (if you make mistakes on your résumé, I can't imagine how you'll be in the office)
- Date gaps in their employment history (it means they probably got fired)
- A lot of jumping around from job to job (i.e., less than one-year of tenure per job)
- No current position (so they're unemployed), or they're currently "self-employed"

You're not allowed to ask any personal questions that could be deemed as prejudice, so nothing regarding age or marital status or religion. But if an applicant is currently unemployed, there is no harm in asking why.

Same thing if there are gaps in their employment history. There is nothing wrong with asking why they left a job without another lined up. And if you're hiring for a technical position like development or design, implement some sort of test to gauge their skillset.

If someone is desperate enough for a job, it isn't unheard of for them to take the work of others and pass it off as their own, and I experienced that myself with a graphic design candidate whose portfolio was filled with work that I knew they did not do. Skilled, competent employees are valuable and sought after, and so typically if a candidate has gaps in their job history, short tenure at various positions and/or is currently unemployed, that's usually a big red flag and you may run into issues if you hire them.

Doing your due diligence on a candidate and trying to prevent a bad hire takes time and experience to do well, but it's never perfect.

You might hire someone that you think is a rock star who ends up crashing and burning inside three months. Or you might decide to give a chance to someone that you're on the fence about, and they end up knocking it out of the park. It costs you time and money every time you have to recruit, interview, hire and train someone new, and so it should be your goal every time to bring in good people that will give you years of tenure, and the best way to do that is to look for red flags on their résumé, ask the right questions, and properly test candidates to confirm their skillset.

Here's a great story to cement my point.

One of the divisions of my company was focused on technical development and content creation and was in the market for a new Senior Developer.

The way we typically recruited company-wide was that my division manager would recruit and interview each candidate, and once they felt they were worthy of the job, I would interview them for the final green light.

I had two people in charge of this division at the time, Myles and Layla. On one occasion, they came into my office excited about a candidate and touted their related work experience. I have to tell you the candidate's name because it's part of the story; his name was Kamal. I looked at his résumé for all of ten seconds before declaring, "He got fired." I sensed it based on the short amount of time that he'd worked at his last company, combined with the fact that he was currently unemployed, meaning he didn't voluntarily leave that job for a new one.

Myles was adamant that Kamal wasn't fired from his previous job, but rather he had finished up a game development project and was subsequently laid off. So, I met with Kamal.

First impression, he came for the interview in a hooded sweatshirt and blue jeans. Now I'm the last guy to talk about fashion and am a big believer in letting people dress casually at the office so long as they're not meeting clients. But when you know you're meeting with the CEO and decision-maker about a job and don't care enough to at least wear business casual attire, why should I care about you?

I asked Kamal why he left his last job, and he said he was laid off. I asked how many people were included in that round of layoffs, and he said two. My hunch immediately was that this person was fired.

From there, I asked him his salary expectations, and he answered, "We already discussed that the last time," and he pointed at Myles. At this point the gloves were ready to come off as I sat forward in my chair, looked him in the eye and said, "Well I sign the checks, so if anybody needs to know, it would be me."

Once the interview wrapped up and I met with Myles and Layla, I told them rather bluntly that this candidate was an "asshole." He showed disrespect with his choice of attire for the interview, he showed disrespect by not wanting to tell me his salary expectations, and I believed he lied about why he left his last position. He was an abrasive personality, and I didn't feel he would mesh with our team.

Myles was adamant that Kamal had the skillset they required, and that I wouldn't have to work with him day-to-day, he would be Myles' problem. So, I told him fine, he's your problem. If you think he's good, and we need him, make the offer.

Within a few weeks after Kamal started with us, I was hearing stories around the office about how rude he was and that he was hoarding candy bars and other snacks from the kitchen, stocking up his desk drawers, and even taking some home. The team had even given him the nickname "Kamal You Can Eat"—now you know why I shared his name!

Worse still, his actual work was subpar, and I came to learn afterwards that as part of the vetting process my team never actually had him complete a related test. So, I made the call to fire him, and taught Myles and Layla the lesson that what someone says on paper does not necessarily reflect the truth.

On another occasion, Myles and Layla brought me another candidate for the same job. They claimed she was personable and had the ideal skillset, and so I met her and learned that she was a relatively new immigrant from India and had moved to Canada along with her husband and new baby. She talked a lot about how her husband needed her to do this, and her husband needed her to do that.

Now some may find this discriminatory, but it's a fact, and I'm being honest—in the Indian culture, at least at the time, it was widely believed that the role of women in society was to be a good mother and wife. And according to an Ipsos Global Trends survey in 2017, over 18,000 adults were polled across twenty-two countries and 64 percent of Indian people believed just that. (Emes 2017)

I've never passed on a qualified candidate based solely on background, religion, or gender, and so I told Myles and Layla the candidate was personable and likeable, so if you believe she has the skillset, you can offer her the job, but understand that given her background and the fact she's a new mother, her husband and her child will always come first before her job, and I'd had problems arise from this in the past.

So, we hired the candidate for the position, and on her very first day—matter of fact, within two hours on her very first day, she got up from her desk and left the office. Layla came to me confused and said, "I think she just quit." But then another member of that team informed us that the woman had told him something about a birthday party before leaving. So, I told Layla to e-mail her, tell her sorry the job didn't work out, and that she would be paid for one full day of work.

The candidate responded to Layla and said no she didn't quit; she just had to go home and bake a cake for her child's birthday party, but that she'd be back at work tomorrow. Sounds crazy perhaps, but it was true. So, I told Layla to politely inform her that she wasn't welcome back.

Sometimes the red flags with a job candidate are so obvious, they reveal themselves during the interview process like a bright neon sign flashing over their heads.

Once again, this story has to do with our efforts hiring a Developer for our tech team—do I detect a pattern here?!? By this point, the manager of the team was a smart, experienced guy named Donald. One day he came into my office with a smile on his face, and so I knew he had a story to tell.

Donald told me that he had interviewed a candidate for a Full-Stack Developer role who he felt had the qualifications for the job. But then the candidate decided to e-mail Donald to rate him on his interview skills. That's right, the candidate told his prospective manager what kind of grade he felt Donald had earned when interviewing the candidate. It was clear what kind of personality we'd be dealing with, so that one was an easy pass.

THE STORYTELLING SALESMAN

When I created Fightful.com I spoke to several candidates for the Managing Editor position. One of them was a person with a lot of notoriety in the world of professional wrestling news, and I initially thought that it would be a coup for me to get them for my website. But on our first phone call, before they even said "hello" to me, the very first words out of their mouth were, "You can't afford me."

I was taken aback by that comment, and instantly disinterested in working with that person. They didn't know me or anything about my background, and so making such an arrogant, if not insulting, comment gave me enough insight into what it would be like dealing with them on a day-to-day basis that I immediately chose to look elsewhere.

The Fightful championship belt that I commissioned Wildcat Belts—same company that makes WWE titles—to produce.

Balls Deep and the Never Were's

These stories are too good not to share, and they exemplify how invaluable it is to be a good interviewer not just in terms of judging someone's character, but also in being able to determine whether someone will be a good personality fit for the team.

While working in sales for Incentaclick, I became very close to one of the company's founders named Sebastian, who I still like and respect to this day.

Interviewing was not Sebastian's strong suit. He never involved me in the interview process until I became Director of Sales later, and he tended to tell me matter-of-factly whenever he hired a new salesperson just before their start date. It led to a rotating door of quite the cast of characters, and I think he typically would hire whoever applied just to fill a seat quickly.

One day I was sitting at my desk when Sebastian introduced me to someone he had just interviewed and hired, a woman who happened to be Israeli just as he was, which is probably why he hired her. After a brief hello, she started speaking to him in Hebrew in front of the whole team, and they went on to have a lengthy conversation that none of us could understand, which I thought made for a bad first impression.

After she left, Sebastian excitedly called me into his office to get my thoughts on her. I told him that I wasn't sure she'd fit in well with the team, which surprised him. He then touted her sales experience and potential, and I assured him we'd give her a chance.

Prior to her first official day, Sebastian had already decided to send her to an upcoming sales conference. And this is where everything quickly came to a head. He had a difficult time just getting her to agree to a flight itinerary. She would complain about the airline or the flight times. Somewhere along the way, I think they mutually decided that this relationship wouldn't work out, and so she never actually started the job.

On another occasion, Sebastian again told me he'd hired a new salesperson. This time, Sebastian decided that the person's first day wouldn't be in the office, but rather at an industry conference in Chicago. And I wasn't aware of this until I met him on the tradeshow floor.

I couldn't understand why you would want someone who didn't know your company or your industry to represent you in front of prospective clients. And I guess that employee felt the same way, because when we got back home after the conference, he decided to quit on what would have been his first official day in the office.

This last one I have told many times to many people. In case this offends anybody just remember—they were his words, not mine!

Anyway, it started off with the usual pattern—Sebastian told me he'd hired a new salesperson. Sebastian wouldn't be in the office the morning that the new guy was starting, and neither would Jack, my direct boss, so the new hire was told to ask for me.

That morning, in strolls this guy with his shirt almost fully unbuttoned wearing a bunch of gold chains with super gelled-up hair. He looked like he'd walked off the set of *Jersey Shore* or something. He introduced himself and said he'd been told to ask for me.

Within about thirty seconds I knew that he would not be a good fit for the team. So I told him to go over and introduce himself to the rest of the group—and then I watched, and I listened.

One of the first questions he asked a co-worker was what the office hours were, since I guess he hadn't been told by Sebastian before he started. He was given the answer of 10:00 a.m. to

6:00 p.m. He then said the words that would immortalize him with our group: "6:00 p.m.? Normally by 6:00 p.m. I'm balls deep into some broad." I saw the jaws of some of the people drop, and I knew that we were done here.

I called Sebastian, no answer. I called my direct manager, Jack, no answer. I then e-mailed both, told them what happened, and said that whether I had the authority to fire anybody or not, if neither one of them arrived by noon, I was firing the guy. I believe it was Jack who arrived first later that morning, and the tenure of Mr. Balls Deep with our company came to a quick end.

Think about the time and the money that would have been saved with a more in-depth interview process. The objective should not be to just fill a seat. And the qualifications should not just be related to industry experience or an education. The right personality and the right fit for the office culture should be a starting point.

———■———

15

Pay Everyone Else Before You Pay Yourself

IT MIGHT BE YOUR IDEA THAT ENABLED YOU TO START YOUR BUSIness, or your capital, or your acumen, but no business is a one-person operation.

Whether it be staff, or vendors, or services, you will undoubtedly surround yourself with people that depend on you to pay them and pay them on time. And as your business grows, and you generate revenue and see money in the bank, you might be tempted to dip into that cash and reward yourself for the time, money, and sacrifices you've made to get to that point. But without those people, you have no business, and so you must be smart and ensure that everyone else is paid for work completed first.

When I started my business, our credit terms with our clients were anywhere from "net seven" to "net thirty," meaning we'd be paid between seven and thirty days from the date an invoice was issued, and that was industry standard. However, our traffic partners, which were one of our primary expenses, had expected credit terms in the "net one" to "net three" range. That meant that we were called upon to float the cash in between the time we paid those vendors and the time we got paid back by our clients.

In those early days, there wasn't a lot of cash to go around. It would have been very easy for us to make up excuses and pay our traffic partners late to keep that float in our pockets and wait until our client payments came in to then pay our vendors. But your reputation means everything in business, especially when you're starting out.

No matter the industry you're in, it's a small world, everybody is connected, and word gets around. If you establish the reputation of paying late, or short-paying, or not paying at all, the next thing you know you'll be reaching out to new vendors who won't return your calls.

Prior to starting my own company, I'd also dealt with employers who made changes to my commission structure on more than one occasion, cutting the percentages or increasing the target revenue numbers each time. Obviously, their objective was to pay me and my co-workers less, not to encourage us to drive more revenue.

When I got some authority as Director of Sales at Incentaclick, I would sometimes have to push back on management who would want me to change my team's commission structure.

I remember once when I was forced to make a change, but I was able to get management to agree to a lesser percentage reduction than they'd wanted. When I informed my team, one of them said that I'd "screwed them" and let them down, not knowing how much I'd pushed back and that if I hadn't, the decrease would have been a lot more significant. I always kept that to myself, so if she ever reads this—now you know!

Given those experiences, I had decided upon launching my company to offer a compensation package among the most aggressive in our industry, and it always remained that way.

Many times, my accountants would tell me how they felt some employees were being paid too generously and that we could immediately increase our profits by cutting the compensation structure and still pay out generous commissions. But I was adamant that I wouldn't change it and had seen and heard enough stories from my time in the advertising sales world to understand the potential repercussions of such a decision.

In the summer of 2013 I went to Philadelphia, Pennsylvania, for an industry conference known as Affiliate Summit East on behalf of my own business. While there I got a text message from a colleague asking if I'd like to meet for a drink.

Historically I've always built better business relationships over a pint at a bar than in a boardroom or on the conference floor, and my colleague knew that. So we met for a drink, and he brought a co-worker with him. They both worked for a competitor; however, I'd known my colleague for many years, and he was a friend regardless of where he worked or the competitive nature of our two companies.

For the next several hours, I listened as my colleague's co-worker complained openly about their employer. I didn't know this co-worker personally, but I knew of him; he was known to be one of the top salespeople at his company. Understanding the value of a competent, skilled salesperson with an established book of business, I was taken aback to hear about how his employer had not only cut his commission percentage on several occasions, but had also offered him performance bonuses based on hitting certain targets, only to renege on paying those bonuses once the targets were achieved.

These stories would be echoed years later by others at that company. One person told me, after one commission restructuring, that the explanation given was that the owners wanted to increase their profits to make them look more attractive to a prospective buyer, at the expense of their employees no less. And another person, after hitting his targets and not being paid his promised bonus, was told that the bonus had been promised by a manager who was no longer with the company and supposedly didn't have the authority to promise it, and so the bonus was essentially null and void.

Not surprisingly, many seasoned members of that team had subsequently quit, sometimes without another job lined up as they couldn't bear the frustration of working there any longer.

It also wasn't uncommon for someone to reach out to me for a prospective job and share similar stories about their previous employer. And this phenomenon of course isn't isolated to the digital marketing world. In fact, recently I caught an episode of a popular reality show about failing restaurants, in which the staff complained about how their boss had cut their hourly wages due to slow business, but still found a way to take multiple vacations per year and drive an expensive car.

It's amazing to me how many business owners and decision makers have such little foresight and only think about today, not tomorrow.

Cutting your staff's compensation plan for no legitimate, viable reason can not only result in a demoralized, disinterested employee who begins to coast at work, but it can cost you a lot of long-term money both directly and indirectly.

Directly, you risk the employee telling your clients, vendors, and competitors as many had told me about their employers, thereby damaging your company's reputation and potentially costing you business. You also risk the employee cutting side deals—such as kickbacks from vendors in exchange for accepting lower pricing—or turning away business out of spite, or quitting.

Indirectly you risk the headache of not only having to rehabilitate your company's reputation and save eroding business, but also the headache of having to recruit, hire, and train new employees to replace those who left you.

And it's hard to put a value not just on someone's experience and portfolio but on their tenure as well. If I can have one good, high-performing salesperson with me for ten years but I must pay them handsomely, is that not worth more than having a rotating door of people that last a year or two on the cheap? Absolutely it is.

Deciding on someone's compensation package should not be done on a whim and not without proper thought and number-crunching. Because again, the last thing you want to do is reduce the percentages after the fact if you aim too high or impact their motivation if you aim too low. So give it proper thought, make sure it's something you can live with both in good times and in bad, and then stick with it.

An Unbelievable Story about Paying for Not Paying

One of my first clients when I ventured out on my own was an old colleague of mine named Ryan. He previously worked for a former client where he had been my day-to-day contact, but now he had started his own business.

Ryan didn't have the greatest reputation in our industry, but I personally had never had an issue with him. Don't get me wrong, I knew he was a bullshitter. One time we were having drinks, and I happened to have a bottle of weight loss supplements that another client was selling and had given to me as a sample. Ryan opened the bottle, took one whiff, and then professed to be such an expert on pharmaceuticals that he could list all the ingredients just by smelling the bottle. As I said, quite the bullshitter. But he hadn't wronged me with respect to business, at least he hadn't yet.

I tend to treat people based on their professional history with me rather than rumors or hearsay of how they treated others, and so I opted to do business with Ryan. He had a product line he was looking to market, and I had demand from our traffic partners. But I kept him on a short leash until I felt more comfortable and extended him a small $5,000 credit limit. He skipped out on the first bill, we ceased doing business, and we lost touch.

Time passed, and I started hearing from a friend who worked for Ryan about issues she was having. She told me her paychecks were coming late, business was down, and some suspicious looking individuals had been visiting their office. It was like a movie; she said those people spoke Russian and would order her to leave her desk so that they could go through her computer. She was concerned about her job and about the situation she might be in.

Sometime after that, I got a phone call with shocking news—Ryan had been shot and killed during a meeting, presumably with the same individuals.

Details are still sketchy, but from what I've heard, Ryan had gone into business with people associated with an organized crime syndicate. He was supposedly late on payments to them, meanwhile he would post photos on social media of himself in a new car, or at his luxury residence, or with a fancy new watch. As the story goes, his business partners were supposedly aware of the photos and aware of his lifestyle and felt that money owed to them was being spent elsewhere, and so they reacted. There was a meeting somewhere in upstate New York, it got heated, and then one of those individuals pulled out a gun and killed Ryan before also taking his own life.

Of course, this was an unusual situation, and it's unlikely that you'll deal with such consequences if you choose to pay your vendors and staff late—not unless they're part of the mob anyway!

The Money Magically Appears!

A couple of years into my sales job at Incentaclick, I was generating big revenue numbers for the company's owners, far more than anyone else on the sales team. I'd also come to learn that our commission structure wasn't as aggressive as some of our competition.

I didn't expect my boss to revamp their whole structure just for me, and so I asked him on a few occasions for a raise in my base salary. Each time I was told that it wasn't in the budget, an excuse that I felt was bullshit given the revenue figures.

When I had negotiated the terms of my employment, I had gotten the company to remove the non-solicitation and non-compete clauses, meaning I was free to jump to another company whenever I wanted. I had friends working for a competitor, and so the owners there got wind of the fact that I had no contractual limitations, and they started pursuing me about making a move.

I really had no desire to leave, because I'd helped my employer build their company from the ground up, I was making pretty good money, and I had the owners in my back pocket and could pretty much come and go as I pleased. But I also knew I was being denied a raise not because the money wasn't there and not because I didn't deserve it, but because they simply didn't want to pay it. So, I had a meeting with this competitor.

After taking me through the typical "song and dance" process, they asked me what it would take to get me to come over.

Now at the time, I was making a $50,000 base salary, but with commission my annual income was in the low six-figure range. That might sound like a lot, but I was generating eight figures in monthly sales for the company at the time. Again, I really didn't want to leave, but I didn't want to burn bridges with any prospective new employers either. So, I threw out a figure that I thought would make them balk and allow us to part amicably—a base salary of $130,000 plus commission. To my surprise, they took the deal and started drafting the paperwork.

I had a bittersweet feeling as I told my employers that I had an offer too good to pass up and would be moving on. And wouldn't you know, within twenty-four hours, they doubled my base salary and promoted me to Director of Sales, a title I didn't even want or ask for. That made my decision easy in the end since I hadn't wanted to leave anyway, I just wanted my compensation to match my worth. Isn't it funny though how they supposedly had no money in the budget for a raise, but once I had one foot out the door, suddenly the money was there.

———■———

16

Knowing When to "Eat Shit"

I'LL NEVER FORGET A MEETING I ONCE HAD WITH MY OLD Incentaclick manager, Jack. The two of us weren't getting along, and so he called a meeting to talk about it.

I've always remembered something that he said to me. He said when it comes to the top producers, he knew he had to "eat shit" sometimes. What he meant was, you must be more tolerant and more flexible with your top revenue generators than with other members of your team.

As I've stated, a competent, skilled salesperson is incredibly valuable to your business, if not invaluable. And so, every place I've ever worked, including my own company, the top salespeople always had a longer leash than everybody else. And that's fine, but the last thing you want to do is blatantly advertise to everyone else who you favor.

When I worked for Yahoo, I was often successful in tracking down and collecting on overdue accounts that were well into the six-figures, whereas the HotJobs Canada sales team in our office would typically land small five-figure deals. It didn't matter to the executives in our office how large a balance I collected on old money versus how small the sales team's deals were in comparison, because sales were sales—they were generating new revenue, I wasn't, so they got the attention, and they got the perks.

In retrospect when I think about some of the actions that I took because of that mistreatment—long morning breakfast breaks, the expensive company lunch etc.—the fact that I got away with everything unscathed tells me that in a small way, my managers were "eating shit" from me because I was a productive employee even if I wasn't directly responsible for new revenue.

Myself and two former co-workers in front of the
Yahoo sign at company headquarters.

THE STORYTELLING SALESMAN

After I hired Sean Ross Sapp as the Managing Editor of Fightful, I started doing a weekly live podcast with him now known as *Fightful's The Hump* on Wednesday afternoons. In addition to that, I oversaw the money and the major business decisions, but otherwise I left the day-to-day operations up to him.

As time went on, and as Fightful started becoming successful, and Sean started getting notoriety in that world, it was noticeable to me how he changed somewhat with respect to how he talked to me not just off the air but also on our live podcasts together.

One of my office staff commented to me once about how she was uncomfortable with how Sean spoke to me on the air. He could be a little quick tempered and aggressive at times and even used coarse language on occasion when addressing me. I knew that that was his personality, and his intention was not to disrespect me, but I also knew the importance of optics, especially given that other employees watched that podcast, and no one ever spoke to me in that manner day-to-day.

I told Sean, and I told the employee, that I considered the podcast to be entertainment and not real life, and so I would tolerate language that others may view as disrespect—up to a point anyway. But I made clear to Sean that behind the scenes, while I always wanted him to speak freely and never be afraid to share his opinion—which is how I like everybody on my payroll to be—I wouldn't tolerate disrespectful conduct. At times Sean can be a little abrasive on day-to-day matters, and he tends to push back a lot, but I chalk it up as another case of "eating shit" for a top producer as he can be aggressive, but never abusive or reprehensible.

Fightful became, and continues to be, a great success due to both of us—I provided the platform, the resources, some key business ideas, and the creative freedom, and Sean put in the work. Time has allowed us to understand each other and how we do business, and our relationship has evolved positively as a result.

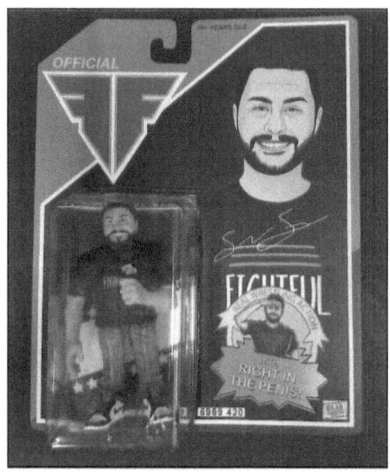

The custom action figure that I had commissioned of Fightful's Sean Ross Sapp. The card was designed by renowned independent wrestler LuFisto!

It wasn't uncommon for the top salespeople at my company to inform me at the last minute that they were going on vacation the following week "but would be available by phone if needed." Or to not show up at the office, only to text me saying they'd be working from home that day. Or to come back from a business conference with an exorbitant expense report that included the finest restaurants and even prime seats at sporting events. These were salespeople generating six or seven figures of monthly gross profits for my business. And so usually I would accept these situations as the cost of doing business, even begrudgingly at times.

It's one thing to "eat shit" for your top producers, but it's another thing to know when to "eat shit."

Optics are important, as is public perception within the office. Everybody talks, and everybody has a pretty good understanding of who makes the most money. What you don't want to do is disrespect and degrade your entire team by rubbing that fact in their faces.

THE STORYTELLING SALESMAN

While I was always more lenient with my top revenue generators and gave them a longer leash, I typically would try to not make it too obvious. I would approve of extra vacation days or turn a blind eye with respect to their expense reports. But if they ever came in late or left early with consistency, I would call them out on it. If they ever gave attitude to people in other departments, I would call them out on it. Or if they took exceptionally long lunch breaks, they would hear from me about it.

And I would never, ever throw a company party for one team only and exclude other teams, because every department contributes to the success of your organization. You can have the greatest salesperson in the world, but if you don't have competent Account Managers, or accounting staff, or designers, or developers, or other support staff, you will only get so far.

One other note about perception: job titles. I don't know if it's the social media generation and people's desire for reassurance and praise from strangers, but I've personally witnessed how much importance some people place on job titles. I've even seen people pass on a raise in their salary in exchange for what they deem to be a better job title.

I have never cared about my job title in any position, ever. All I ever cared about was how much money I made.

When I started my company, we created a corporation and were told by our attorney that we had to have a Chief Executive Officer (CEO) and a Chief Operating Officer (COO). My partner Luke and I didn't care about job titles, and so I asked our lawyer if we could just be "Janitor 1" and "Janitor 2." And if he had said yes, we would have gone with that. But he said we couldn't, and so I became CEO not because I asked for it, but because it was a corporate requirement.

When I worked at Incentaclick, a co-worker once requested to add "Senior" to their title in lieu of a salary increase. At the next weekly meeting, management announced the new job title, and the co-worker couldn't have looked prouder. But I just thought to myself, I would have pushed for more money instead.

At my own company, we had a very competent finance person who I had rewarded with raises on several occasions. She would often push for me to change her title to something more senior. I was reluctant to do so, because she dealt with our corporate accountants who would tell me how smart she was, but that she was inexperienced and needed time. But in terms of compensation, she earned as much as anyone with the other title.

One day she received a job offer elsewhere with an aggressive salary increase. I told her I don't do bidding wars, but I would match that offer one time because she was a valued employee. The other company countered at a higher salary, so I told her to take it. She did, and I then hired a new person who happened to have a lot more corporate experience in the field, and so I agreed to give them the job title that the other person had wanted.

Eventually, I heard that the job didn't work out for the former employee at the other place of business. And then Luke told me that she texted him, apparently unhappy that we had given the new hire the job title that she had wanted. And keep in mind, her new salary had she stayed would have been higher than what the new person made. It showed me again how much importance some people place on a job title.

Always take the money. The ability to pay your bills and live a comfortable lifestyle is a lot more important than public perception.

17

Money Out > Money In = Bad

OVER THE YEARS I'VE SEEN AND HEARD ABOUT A LOT OF COMPANIES going out of business. And you'll always hear various excuses for it. Change in the market. Recession. Partners split up. Competitor ate up the market share. When it comes right down to it though, there's usually one basic reason and that is quite simply, the money out exceeded the money in.

You can expect to wear many hats when running a business, especially in the early days. But no matter how busy I got, I made time every day to check the bank accounts, and twice a week I would review our accounts receivable (AR) and get payment updates from my sales and accounting teams. For any business to survive and thrive over the long haul, cash flow should be king, and AR should be queen of your "corporate kingdom" so to speak.

Even though I did no formal budgeting, I always had a pretty good idea of our financials, not just monthly, but weekly or even daily. I always focused on gross profit more so than top-line revenue because gross profit would help me gauge expected cash flow for major fixed expenses like rent and payroll.

At the end of a quarter when it came time to issue our dividends, which were predominantly how my partner and I got paid, I would always look at cash flow, look at the AR, look at the expected major costs over the coming weeks, and issue an appropriate dividend that left a significant cash buffer in case something unexpected occurred. Just in case we ran into a situation with a client paying a bill late, or a marketing cost spiking that would subsequently increase that expense, or an opportunity arising to acquire a company, or launch a new business unit, or anything else that would require additional cash, I always made sure we had it available.

Every quarter I would ensure that there was significant money left in the bank after issuing dividends. And several times a client would skip out on a bill, and we'd have to go the legal route which can take months, meaning there was less cash on hand than expected. That in turn meant that we'd have to take a smaller dividend and maybe no dividend at all. But never, ever did we neglect the AR and let unpaid debts escalate out of hand or deplete the company cash reserves to line our own pockets.

The same can't be said for some other companies, where it seems that lifestyle and public perception are more important than the health of the business, especially in the social media era. I've seen a lot of company owners post photos of themselves in their new Ferrari, or on their company jet, or wearing their new Rolex when in reality it's a friend's car, they leased the jet, their bank accounts are in overdraft, their credit is maxed out, they're late paying their vendors, and their business is hanging by a thread, but all is well according to Instagram.

THE STORYTELLING SALESMAN

This perception doesn't just end with the business owner. Sometimes this perception starts with the client, and the business owner ends up holding the bag as a result.

When I worked at Incentaclick, my biggest client at one time was a young man named Declan. He had made his fortune through various Internet businesses and was now looking to conquer the online marketing space in the health and beauty sector and had a product line he was looking to market. He bought out several of his competitors to secure market share, and I believe that he manipulated his campaigns so that one would convert better with us, and another would convert better with a competitor. I think he did this to ensure that the top marketing companies in that industry would all need him.

Declan put a lot of effort into developing the reputation of being a high-rolling, globetrotting somebody. I have a few interesting stories about him.

In 2009 we were in Las Vegas for an industry conference known as Affiliate Summit West. At the time, XS Nightclub at the Encore hotel and casino was the newest and hottest club in Vegas. I was not a club guy by any means, but Declan asked me to meet him there on a Saturday night, and I was going to oblige my biggest client.

I showed up, and Declan had a large entourage with him. He approached the front desk and asked for tables in a prime location in the club along with several bottles of their best champagne. The employee told him that it was Saturday night, he had no reservation, and the club was fully booked so no tables were available. Declan then repeated his ask, but this time, he pulled out a large stack of $100 bills from his jacket pocket. The employee looked at the money, said, "One moment," and left to go speak to somebody. When they returned, they informed Declan that magically, they could suddenly accommodate us.

As a long-time pro wrestling fan, I couldn't help but be reminded of some television segments from decades earlier featuring "Million Dollar Man" Ted DiBiase doing basically the same thing. But this was not scripted entertainment, this was real life. Or at least, some semblance of real life.

What happened next was like a scene in a movie. Declan requested that before we were escorted to our tables, they turn the music off, turn the lights up, and then play the song *The Champ Is Here* by Jadakiss. Each bottle of champagne was placed in a bucket that had pyrotechnics coming out of it, and each bucket was held high in the air by a club waitress and carried to our tables. Our group then followed the waitresses and the pyrotechnics and made our way to our tables as all the club patrons watched in silence. Maybe Declan loved it, but I felt kind of stupid.

It just so happened that a friend of mine was at the club, and she knew I had planned to go, but she didn't know I was part of that group. She texted me to ask if I was there and told me that she was in an upstairs booth alongside legendary rapper Snoop Dogg. She then recited the words that Snoop had said out loud when Declan led the way in, and I still smile when I think about it. Snoop allegedly said, "Who the hell is this asshole?"

Another time, Declan brought his private jet all the way from the West Coast out to visit us in Toronto and took the entire sales team on a short flight to a vineyard just outside Niagara Falls for the day. My boss and I then flew back out west with him on his jet to spend a couple days and get some business done. We were treated to fine restaurants and a nice hotel.

I believe that Declan intentionally created this persona for himself so that the owners of the various marketing companies he worked with, including Incentaclick, would extend him unlimited credit lines thinking he was a multimillionaire entrepreneur with an endless supply of cash. And it worked. I was told by management that Declan's campaigns had an unlimited budget, and we could generate as many sales as possible. But by 2010 I started to hear rumblings from friends at competitive businesses that Declan was late with his payments.

Management at Incentaclick always kept me in the dark and wouldn't give me access to the books, and so I didn't know how much credit we had extended Declan and how often he was paying. What I knew was that we were generating six figures worth of sales revenue every day on Declan's campaigns, and so were our top competitors. I also knew that there were problems because whenever it was time to submit payroll, someone from accounting would come to me asking me to follow up with Declan's team on payment, and so I suspected that without those payments, we would risk being unable to cover payroll. I would ask our CEO if we should pause Declan's campaigns, and I'd be told no, all is well, and keep it going.

Next, I started hearing from some of Declan's disgruntled employees who had either already left his business or were about to. They would tell me about how they hadn't been paid what they'd been promised, and they warned me to be wary of the situation. They told me that among other claims, that private jet was allegedly leased, not owned. All part of the well-crafted persona.

Eventually I learned that Declan had unpaid invoices with us in the mid-seven figure range. And we weren't alone. At least two of our top competitors were owed similar amounts. Then one day, my CEO came to me and happily announced that Declan had summoned the heads of the top marketing networks, including Incentaclick, to a black-tie affair at his home over the weekend. I wasn't invited, and that was okay with me. I was also skeptical about whether this event would result in those invoices getting paid.

The following Monday I met with my CEO, and he couldn't contain his excitement as he told me the story.

Picture the scene—the bosses of all these marketing companies from the industry are gathered at Declan's luxury condo.

The elevator opens, and from it emerges a couple of gentlemen in black suits wearing earpieces. As it was described to me, they looked like members of the U.S. Secret Service. And apparently, as it turned out, they *were* members of the U.S. Secret Service.

After scouring the scene and declaring the area to be safe, up came Declan's special guests for the party—none other than former U.S. Presidents George H.W. and George W. Bush. Yup, Declan had booked the former Presidents to impress clients that he owed tens of millions of dollars to combined.

Over the next several hours, my CEO mingled and took photos with the two Georges. And he happily showed me pictures on his phone of him posing with them. I half-jokingly asked, "Did he give you a check?" in reference to Declan's outstanding bills. Of course, he didn't. But that dinner had worked, because my CEO had a renewed faith that the money would be paid, and that Declan was the real deal and would become a strategic partner once again.

Well, the money was never paid. And Incentaclick eventually went out of business, in large part because of the repercussions of that balance going unpaid. Several of our competitors who were also owed a large sum also went out of business. Again, the money out exceeded the money in.

Declan went quiet for a while, but a few years later he resurfaced. And he must have heard that by that time I owned one of the largest online marketing companies in that industry because he reached out, but he did so through an intermediary, not directly. He was again launching a product line in the health and beauty space and was looking to market it. I made it clear that I would only work with Declan on a pre-payment basis, meaning he'd have to pay in advance. He obviously wasn't interested, and that was that.

Most businesses have their ebbs and flows. You'll have times that are great, and you might have times that aren't so great. So it's imperative that you keep an eye on your cash, gauge your monthly expenses, ensure that the money in exceeds the money out, ensure there's a good buffer of cash to cover anything unexpected, and monitor your AR. Because if you get in the habit of paying yourself a fixed amount regardless of the state of your business, or if you believe that some of your clients are a bigger deal than maybe they really are, you could run into trouble in a hurry.

Gaining Through Saving

Having my website revenue nosedive in my younger days turned out to be a blessing in disguise, because it not only helped me appreciate the value of a dollar, but it also helped me learn to save and be frugal with what little money I had. And that became an invaluable skillset once I had my own company to run.

I went through a difficult time in my life financially in the early 2000s while still in my twenties. My parents would send me cash in the mail to help cover my rent. I would look for family meal deals from the local pizzerias, keep the food in the freezer, and stretch it out to last me an entire week. And I must have been quite the catch, because every story I remember about a girl I dated at that time involves me being broke!

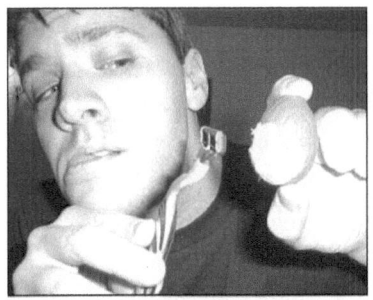 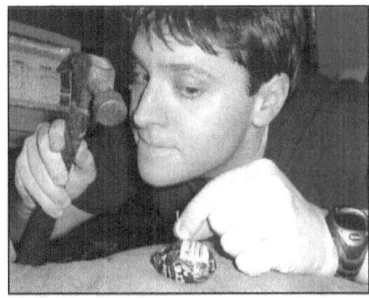

In early 2002 I was so broke, I even entered a contest promoted by Cadbury to determine the most creative way to get the filling out of a chocolate egg, with a cash prize at stake. I didn't win.

One time, it was her birthday. She was expecting a nice dinner out, and I had no clue how I would pay for it. I had little cash in the bank, and my credit card was maxed out. At that time, I used to buy a lottery ticket every week, and as luck would have it, I won a thousand dollars in the lottery the week of her birthday. So she got her nice dinner, plus I got to play the big shot by pulling out a wad of cash from my pocket.

But despite going through a rough patch with minimal income, I made it through in large part because I spent as little as I could day-to-day, and I tried to minimize my debts.

The number-one financial liability that most people have after their rent or their mortgage is their credit card debt. According to The Motley Fool, the average credit card balance in the United States in 2021 was $5,221 (Caporal 2022). And according to Forbes.com, the average credit card interest rate on American accounts was 27.99 percent in August 2023 (Frankel 2023). That's a crazy-high number when you consider that you're lucky to find a savings account interest rate above 5 percent. And what a lot of people don't realize is that if you only make the minimum payment that's listed on your monthly credit card bill, you're only covering the interest and not the principal, meaning your balance will never come down.

Even when times were tough, I always tried my best to pay more than the monthly minimum on my credit card or pay it off in full if I could. I also knew not to increase my credit card limit, which was a difficult temptation to avoid in hard times. I knew if I increased the limit, sure I'd have more cash available to spend, but I'd also end up with a higher balance meaning I'd be paying even more interest in months when I couldn't afford to pay the card off. And one piece of advice I'd give someone with credit card debt now is to reduce your limit if you can. As you pay it down, reduce your limit. You won't miss it, you'll be paying less interest, and ultimately, it'll help you pay off the balance quicker.

The other thing I would recommend is that you get a financial advisor, and make sure they're legitimate and accredited. Even if you can only afford to invest a small sum of money at first, at least it's something. Start out investing conservatively until you're comfortable, and do NOT check your balance multiple times a day or even every day, because it's unrealistic to expect returns that fast and you'll drive yourself crazy.

Don't assume that if you make more, you'll automatically save more without being disciplined about your debts. Lifestyle inflation is real, meaning your monthly expenses are likely to increase as you earn more. And we've all heard the stories about young athletes losing control of their newfound wealth and ending up broke in the end. Learning to save and minimize your highest-interest debts first will lead you down the path towards a happy retirement.

Credit Terms vs. Credit Limits

I used to joke with my sales team that I was going to put a big plaque on the wall by their area of the office that said in big letters: "Credit terms and credit limits are not the same thing." Getting them to become cognizant of the latter and not just think about the former was an ongoing problem. Had I not been as aware of it as I was, we would have run into AR issues and big delinquent balances with all our accounts.

Let's clarify the difference. Credit terms—also referred to as payment terms—is the number of days a client has to pay an invoice from the time it's issued. If you have a client on "net thirty" terms, that means an invoice must be paid within thirty days from the date you issue it. It's standard practice to negotiate those terms with every client, and often there are set terms that companies abide by that are deemed the standard in whatever industry they're in.

Credit limits are very different. This is the amount of money that you are willing to essentially loan to a client. It's the amount that you will allow a company to spend with you before they're required to pay it off.

Typically, you would have a prospective client fill out a credit application that includes a bank reference and trade references. You would then contact those references and ask them questions to paint a picture of how liquid your prospective client is, how much money they have, how much they spend, and how fast they usually pay. You would then use that information to determine a credit limit for that client with your company, meaning the amount of money that you are comfortable extending before they're required to pay it back.

On *so* many occasions, I would assign a credit limit to one of my salespeople's accounts, let's say $10,000 for example. And each account would also have agreed upon credit terms, such as "net thirty." Inevitably, the account would hit the $10,000 credit limit, we would issue them an invoice, and I would tell the salesperson to pause their account until they paid. And every single time their response would be, "Why should I pause them, they have thirty days to pay, they're within their credit terms."

Always, always, always, they would ignore the credit limit and focus on the credit terms, because they were trying to prevent me from pausing an account that was making them commission. But if you're not cognizant of the credit limit and allow the account to remain active, next thing you know you've extended them more credit than they can afford, and you're left with a big unpaid balance.

It doesn't matter how much revenue your online reporting system shows. What matters is how much money is in the bank.

Over the years, I have seen several companies go out of business for this very reason. They're too focused on the revenue reflected in their sales platform, and not focused enough on their AR or their bank balance. It seems simple and straightforward, but to many companies I've seen, it might as well be rocket science because they have no comprehension of it at all. Credit terms and credit limits are not the same thing.

18
When It's Time to Cut the Cord

IN THE MOVIE *LITTLE BIG LEAGUE*, A TWELVE-YEAR-OLD KID NAMED Billy inherits the Minnesota Twins baseball team from his grandfather. He names himself the manager, and one day, when his favorite player, a struggling veteran named Jerry, hits a single in a meaningless game, Billy celebrates as if he'd hit a home run in the World Series. He then realizes that Jerry's best days are behind him, and that he had allowed his personal feelings for Jerry to dictate his position in the starting lineup of the team.

We've all been there. You have an employee on your team that you really like, and they're not getting it done, but you keep them on staff hoping they'll manage to turn it around. Or you start a new business venture believing it'll be a runaway hit but months later and a lot of money spent, it still hasn't taken off.

Not only are you wasting time and money with these inadequacies, but there's also an opportunity cost—what are you losing by *not* fixing the problem and potentially turning business around by way of some hard decisions?

I decided to launch a new division for my company in the market research space and hired my old colleague Riley to head it up. It was in an industry I didn't have much experience in, but Riley did, and because I believed in him, coupled with the fact that I liked the idea of creating a proprietary tech asset, and I wanted to diversify our revenue, I went for it.

The plan was to create our own survey panel website where consumers would answer market research questions on behalf of our clients and be rewarded with points that they could exchange for gift cards. Our clients would then pay us for every completed survey we sent them. Consumer survey data is invaluable to brands looking to improve their business, and so we were paid a premium for it.

I did what I normally wouldn't do—I gave Riley the freedom to make hiring decisions as well as outsource development decisions, and I also gave him free rein with respect to the design of the survey panel website, how it would look, what features it would offer, etc. He was the one with the industry experience and knowledge, so I felt I had to trust his judgment.

Riley's first sales hire on that team was an industry veteran whom he knew from that business. I was very skeptical, not just because this fellow was unemployed at the time, but because he had high salary expectations given his experience. But Riley assured me we needed him, so I reluctantly agreed, and we took him on.

Every week we would have meetings, and every week this guy could talk the talk, telling me about the grandiose plans that he had with certain prospective clients. But as the months passed, not one deal got closed.

THE STORYTELLING SALESMAN

I was on Riley incessantly, saying this salesperson was a waste of our time, and we needed to let him go, but Riley always defended him and said that it was difficult for them to get business done when the technology wasn't built yet. Of course, it begged the question, why did Riley want me to hire him so badly if the platform needed to be built first?

These types of inefficiencies and head-scratching decisions were commonplace. Then one day, we had a meeting where the sales guy had his laptop hooked up to the projection screen, and he inadvertently revealed where his focus likely was.

As he went into his e-mail looking for a particular file for a presentation, I couldn't help but notice that his Inbox was loaded with dozens of e-mails about voiceover work. In fact, he had few company-related e-mails in there as the voiceover ones were predominant. I'd heard in the past that he was an aspiring comedian, but now it seemed clear that he was looking for opportunities in the entertainment world.

I met with Riley and told him that I now understood why no business had been closed after almost a year of employment—the job was a means to pay the bills while the salesperson pursued his true aspirations. I took away Riley's free rein, and ordered him to fire the salesperson, and he did.

The time finally came for Riley to present the beta version of our survey panel website that had long been in development. As soon as it appeared on the big screen in the boardroom, I was stunned at how abysmal it was.

In the past, I had given people in other departments the opportunity to train newcomers for the first time, and I found that they sometimes lacked the realization that new hires don't understand certain terminology that to them is common knowledge because they deal with it every day. So as part of the training, they would randomly mention certain words or phrases without explaining what they meant, leaving a newcomer's head spinning.

That is essentially what Riley did with this platform. This was going to be a consumer-facing website, and it needed to be as user-friendly as possible. But Riley designed it in such a way that he understood how it worked and how to navigate it because he built it, but nothing was clearly explained. So, a consumer who was new to the site would have no idea how it worked or what it did, because it wasn't properly laid out. It would have been an epic failure had we launched it in that condition, so I ordered that it be completely overhauled.

Between the sales hire, the beta launch of the platform, and other issues that had arisen over time, I questioned if Riley was the right choice to manage that department, and I even quietly reached out to my network to see the availability of a potential replacement. But everybody has strengths and weaknesses, and while development and design had proved to be weaknesses for Riley, one of his definite strengths was his ability to build relationships. His team liked and respected him, as did his colleagues, and as did I. He was a friend before he was an employee, but that was the mistake.

Much like Billy with Jerry the baseball player, I allowed my personal feelings to get in the way of business. Rather than nip the problem in the bud, I put a band-aid on it—I got other people in my company involved with the project and had them collaborate with Riley. But over time, issues just kept popping up, all of them avoidable and fixable, and all of them caused either directly or indirectly by Riley. On a weekly basis, someone from that team would come to me to vent their frustration over the way he worked.

We launched the redesigned website, and for a while it did well, especially for a small team. It was a high margin business and gave me proprietary technology which is what I'd wanted.

But there was a glaring issue—we were reliant on a single client for almost all the revenue. The success or failure of that platform was dependent on whatever budget that one client gave us.

Finally, everything came to a head when the client refused to pay a large portion of their bills, claiming that most of the consumer leads that we had generated for them were fraudulent. Customers were basically trying to trick the system by signing up under multiple accounts and taking the same surveys repeatedly to earn points and redeem them for those gift cards.

When I questioned Riley about it, he tried to shrug it off saying that consumer fraud was part of the business. But without that client, the revenue dropped to almost nothing. With a laundry list of issues and now no revenue to justify his position, I finally made the difficult decision to let Riley go.

Because I liked Riley and knew he was a genuine guy and family man, I wanted to do right by him. So I covered the costs to send him to a conference in that industry so that he could network and explore new job opportunities, and eventually he did find work elsewhere. We lost touch, which is unfortunately the side effect of mixing business with friendship. I think of him sometimes, and I hope he's doing well.

A similar story involved my mobile development lead, Myles.

It started out the same way—I wanted to diversify our revenue, and I wanted some proprietary assets. Myles and I had worked together in the past but not directly, and so while I'd heard that he worked in web development and knew that he was a well-spoken, articulate person, I didn't have any first-hand knowledge of his skill set.

Myles reached out to me and presented an idea he had for a mobile game. I liked the concept, and we had thought about launching a mobile division because our traffic partners had a surplus of mobile traffic available to market such a product. So I hired Myles to oversee that project. We outsourced the development work initially, with Myles choosing a small local studio comprised of two senior engineers to handle it. But the day-to-day decisions were left up to Myles.

On a regular basis, I would hold meetings with Myles in which he would show me design specs, drawings, and an outline for how the game would function, and I'd make tweaks here and there, but admittedly, I left most of the work up to Myles since he came from that world, and this game was his vision.

Then came the day for the beta launch. I downloaded the game onto my phone and planned to spend time over the course of the weekend testing it out.

I knew very quickly that this game in its current form wouldn't make a dime.

The first problem was that it had a blue color scheme. Every character, every background, everything was blue. I hated it and had brought it up during the design process, but Myles explained that it produced a unique user experience like how the movie *Sin City* utilized the color red. And so, he really pushed for it and believed in it.

But the color was just part of the problem. The game was supposed to feature in-app purchases where users would use real cash to buy virtual currency that they would then spend to unlock certain characters or abilities, and that was how we would make money. In fact, that's how most mobile games make money; you download the game for free and spend real dollars to unlock premium items. But Myles designed the game to give away so much virtual currency and made it so easy to complete levels and subsequently unlock premium items for free, there was no reason to ever buy anything.

The following Monday morning I had a meeting with Myles and told him that the game would have to be completely overhauled because in its present form it would make zero dollars. I started becoming much more involved, including having the developers from the outsourced studio come into the office for regular meetings.

To Myles's credit, he'd found two competent, skilled people who I respected to the point that I eventually hired them full-time. Then one day in a meeting, after we'd already gone well past the deadline both in terms of time and money due to the game overhaul, I asked the developers in front of Myles what they thought of the game they'd built. They answered quite honestly that they didn't think it would succeed, but that they were just following the orders of the client.

Next, I asked them about the blue color scheme, since by this point, we had replaced it with vibrant colors like most games offer. They told me that studies had been done that showed that in video games, blue is known as one of the "sad" colors and can create negative feelings. They again explained that they were just following the orders of the client.

Myles then sealed his fate by joking around about the choice of blue even though it had long been a feature he pushed hard for despite my reluctance. I subsequently made the decision to let him go and worked with the developers and my content team to complete the game. But I realized it would take more time and a lot more money to do it right, and eventually we abandoned it.

In these scenarios with Riley and with Myles, money was wasted, time was wasted, and we went way over budget and deadline. And while Riley's platform was salvaged and ended up making a few bucks, Myles's game didn't—and deep down I knew the game wouldn't succeed even before the beta launch and pressed on anyway.

The fault didn't lie with Riley or with Myles; the fault was mine. I'm the one who decided to enter markets that I wasn't overly familiar with, and I'm the one who gave too much freedom to the heads of those divisions when they needed proper guidance and supervision. It's not unlike Homer Simpson being given the freedom by his half-brother Herb Powell to create a new car that resulted in the monstrosity dubbed "The Homer" that cost so much to produce and warranted such a high retail price that Herb's car manufacturing company went out of business on an episode of *The Simpsons*.

I learned some valuable lessons through these experiences, not only about the risks of being too hands-off and giving an employee too much freedom, but also about knowing when something isn't working and cutting the cord on it. I told myself at the time that I was too busy with my other businesses to devote the necessary time to these projects. But in retrospect, I know that I could have made time, and I know that because, when I saw inefficiencies in the management of those projects, I *did* make time.

Don't let personal feelings or pride get in the way of business decisions. I let Riley and Myles oversee their respective divisions on their own far too long because I liked them personally and had known them both for years, and particularly with the mobile game, I let the project carry on rather than pull the plug on it even after I knew that it wasn't going to work.

It's hard for a businessperson who's been successful in different ventures to accept defeat, which is probably why Vince McMahon unsuccessfully relaunched his XFL football league in 2020 after losing tens of millions the first time around.

When a venture isn't working out, you also need to be open-minded and be willing to pivot and try new ideas to improve your business.

When we started Fightful.com, our primary revenue streams were going to be basically the same as what I had with my original website several years earlier—advertising revenue and merchandise sales from an online ecommerce store. But the online advertising industry had changed as time had passed and people had become oblivious to banner advertising. We subsequently couldn't command ad rates as high as what I had been accustomed to before. And so, for the first couple of years Fightful hemorrhaged money, because our costs greatly exceeded our revenue. And on several occasions, Sean, my Managing Editor, asked me if he'd need to find another job.

By 2018, about two years after our launch, I noticed a change with respect to a lot of online content platforms. Their business model was changing from an ad-based model to a direct-to-consumer (DTC) subscription-based model. Major newspapers like the New York Times for example, went in that direction. Even television distribution started favoring DTC streaming services like Hulu, Peacock, or ESPN+ as cable providers started losing millions of subscribers every year.

This trend was no different in the world of pro wrestling news, and in fact, some of Fightful's competitors had already been using a subscription-based service for several years.

I also noticed that the wrestling fan base—though smaller than it was in the late 1990s when the business seemed to peak behind such names as Stone Cold Steve Austin and The Rock—was willing to spend money on a product that they liked. Fightful was doing a lot of live podcasting on YouTube and many of our devoted viewers would send a donation known as a "superchat" through YouTube that entitled them to ask a question to the podcast hosts and get it read and answered live on the air.

I became convinced that if we created a premium service that featured exclusive news and content that couldn't be found anywhere else, our fan base would support it, and that would be our path to profitability.

There was a membership platform called Patreon that provided content creators with the necessary tools to run a subscription service. Many content creators were earning monthly income through the platform, and in exchange, Patreon would take a percentage of the subscription revenue as their fee. I felt that this would be the easiest and fastest way to launch a premium service and at least test the concept. So I told Sean and the rest of my Fightful team that this was the direction we needed to go.

To this day we still joke about this, but Sean was adamantly against the idea of creating a subscription service. He didn't believe that people would pay money for professional wrestling news. But I disagreed because competitors had already proven it could work, and I believed in the support of our fan base. This was one of the few times that I had to use my authority to overrule Sean and force my idea through. But I assured him that if the service—which I called Fightful Select—was successful, he would be rewarded accordingly.

Within a few years, thanks to Sean's hard work and knack for breaking news stories that were accurate and reliable, Fightful Select became the largest wrestling-related platform on Patreon, more than tripling the subscriber count of the next biggest channel.

Fightful went from a money loser to a profitable venture, and I kept my promise and rewarded Sean handsomely—he ended up making almost ten times what he'd originally asked for when I hired him, plus I gave him a minority ownership stake in Fightful. Sean was instrumental in the success of the website, plus his hard work allowed me to be mostly hands off just as I'd wanted and treat the site as passive income, and so I felt that he deserved it. But if I hadn't recognized that our business model wasn't working and we needed to adjust, we likely wouldn't have gotten to the levels that we've since achieved.

Accept Responsibility and Have Awareness

I think it's human nature for people to not want to admit when they're wrong or take the blame when something doesn't go their way. My wife teases me about my own inability to admit when I'm wrong, or when she's right for that matter! And maybe that's

THE STORYTELLING SALESMAN

okay when you're at home debating about who that actor was you saw make a cameo in a movie. But it's a whole other matter if you're allowing that stubbornness to affect your workplace.

In my late twenties, I promoted some live minor league pro wrestling shows in Ontario, Canada, alongside a couple of partners. We divided up the duties based on our respective skill sets, with me primarily handling talent relations while somebody else managed the booking of venues and the marketing of shows.

Most of our events drew poorly and lost money, and afterwards I found myself blaming the person responsible for the marketing for doing a bad job and being the reason for the poor ticket sales. I even wrote a book about my wrestling experiences entitled *Wrestling's Underbelly: From Bingo Halls to Shopping Malls,* and you might find an eBook version kicking around on the Internet today. It wasn't until years later when I reread that book that I recognized my inability to accept responsibility for those live event failures.

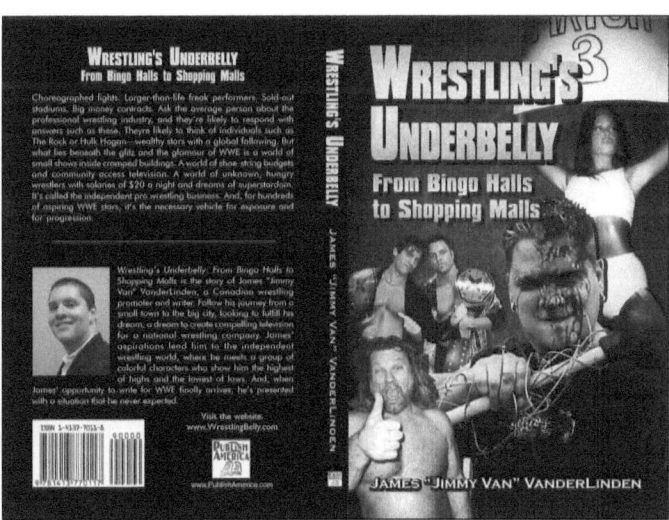

My first book about my experiences in pro wrestling. I might clean it up, update it and release a second edition.

Even though marketing wasn't a task that had been assigned to me, I had a financial interest in those shows, and so I should have been more proactive, kept up on ticket presales, and stepped up to try to improve the numbers. Instead of pointing fingers, I should have admitted my own faults and inefficiencies. You won't improve by tricking yourself into believing that you're always right and others are to blame when something doesn't work out. It's okay to make mistakes—so long as you learn from them to not make them again.

Related yet different topic—be aware of your surroundings, especially if you find yourself in a beneficial position.

When working at Incentaclick in the mid-2000s, we initially had two sales teams. Each team had a manager, with me managing one team, and a long-time friend and colleague managing the other. Eventually our boss decided to merge the two teams and make me the Director of the entire group, meaning my colleague would now report to me. From the get-go I was cognizant of the situation and treated her with kid gloves compared to the others because I knew that if the roles were reversed, I wouldn't have liked it, and so she probably didn't either.

Years later, after launching my company, we had an open-concept layout at the office, and I would occasionally hear the top sales reps boast about their commissions or expensive items they'd purchased, or large stock positions that they had. Meanwhile, their co-workers who made a fraction of what they made would be sitting feet away. Sometimes I would have to tell those salespeople not to talk about money in the office. Everybody had a general idea of what the salespeople made, but that didn't mean you had to throw it in their faces. Be aware.

———■———

19

What's the Benefit?

WE LIVE IN A SOMEWHAT SANITIZED WORLD TODAY IN WHICH PEOPLE are often overly sensitive and easily offended. And unfortunately, we also live in a world in which media illiteracy is widespread. It has become quite common, for example, for someone to read the headline of a story and then react swiftly on social media without reading the article and absorbing all the facts first. This is why anyone in a prominent position—more so than that, anyone with something to lose—needs to think before posting anything online.

Social media has become a necessity in today's world. Consumers have grown accustomed to having the ability to communicate with a service or product owner in real time, not to mention post reviews of those services or products and either praise them or shit on them depending on their experience.

And let's not forget consumption and influence. In GlobalWebIndex's *2020 Social Media Trends* report, they found that social media users were spending an average of two hours and twenty-four minutes per day multi-networking across an average of eight social networks and messaging apps. (Kemp 2020)

As far back as 2014, a survey commissioned by *Variety* found that the five most influential figures among American teenagers were all YouTube celebrities, eclipsing mainstream celebrities from traditional entertainment mediums like movies or music. (Ault 2014) It is integral that every company have some sort of social media presence today, and it's common now to employ full-time staff to oversee these channels. With Fightful.com for example, we have a social media presence that includes channels on X (Twitter), YouTube, Meta (Facebook), Instagram, and TikTok, which are integral to the growth and success of the site.

The question I always ask myself before posting anything, and the question I've recommended that my staff ask themselves in the same position, is simply: "What's the benefit?" What's the benefit to posting versus not posting? What are the pros? What are the cons? And if the cons outweigh the pros, why are you posting it?

One of the first lessons I ever learned in business, even before social media became so prevalent, was to always avoid two issues: politics and religion. Reason being is that you risk dividing your audience. And in today's world, where I own various web entities that have a social media presence, I sometimes have to remind the staff that oversee those entities not to post, like, forward, or re-post anything related to either of those issues.

In today's world, social media etiquette now goes beyond just politics and religion to include social issues as well. And more than that, we've come to learn that smartphones are everywhere and that professional conduct in public is required.

There are dozens of examples of someone behaving inappropriately in a public place, someone else recording video of it on their phone—sometimes unbeknownst to the offending person—that video then going viral on social media, and the offending individual subsequently losing their job or becoming vilified online, receiving death threats to themselves and even their families.

There are also many cases of a business owner or corporate executive posting something ill-timed or in poor taste and subsequently losing vendors, sponsors, employees, and customers. It's important to be aware of yourself and your surroundings and to think twice before you choose to engage with anyone in a public setting, especially online.

Occasionally I'll see someone on my payroll post something that I think could hurt our business, but then you run into another issue—did they post it on their personal account, or on a company account?

If on a company account it's a simple solution—delete, and if necessary, apologize. But if they posted on a personal account, I don't necessarily have the right to tell them to take it down even though the size of their following is probably a result of their affiliation with my platform. However, depending on the severity of what's been posted, it could be grounds for termination. Fortunately, I haven't yet encountered a situation in which someone posted something so severe I was forced to take serious action.

I'm not very active on social media myself, aside from my X (Twitter) account, where I post predominantly about Fightful or one of my other web properties, or my favorite sports such as hockey or pro wrestling. I tend to not personalize anything and leave my family out of the equation. But for all the benefits and all the conveniences that the Internet and social media provide, there's of course a dark side, including the negative, uninformed posts created on a day-to-day basis by Internet trolls—people who are generally unhappy in their lives and looking to trigger a reaction.

A few times over my professional life, negative and untrue claims have been posted online about me, my partners, or my business. People would encourage me to respond and get the truth out. But I would typically choose silence. In the world of social media, if a trolling message doesn't generate a reaction, the fun is gone for the poster, and they usually move on.

The objective of these people is to bring others down and try to make them as miserable as they are. It's human nature to want to defend yourself and to respond to negative and even offensive comments from others online. But there's no benefit. One defensive response will only illicit the next negative comment. So as difficult as it might be, ignore and move on.

20

Selling the Business: Reality vs. Fairy Tale

WE'VE ALL SEEN REALITY TELEVISION SHOWS LIKE *SHARK TANK* OR *Dragon's Den* where budding entrepreneurs get the chance to partner with business tycoons and bring their dreams to life. They negotiate a deal on the air, they shake hands, and then it's smiles and high-fives all around as we cut to commercial break. But did you know that half of the deals that are broadcast on *Shark Tank* never actually close? (Cayasso 2022) There's a lot of paperwork and a lot of red tape that can get in the way of bringing those dreams to fruition.

If you have a business to sell, your prospective buyer will typically fall under one of two categories: they'll either be a strategic buyer or a financial buyer.

A strategic buyer is a company or investor that has an existing portfolio that they believe your business will add synergistic value to. Often, they're in the same industry and target companies that can complement their existing business.

A financial buyer is a long-term investment company that looks to buy a business that they can then manage and grow to increase its value so that they can sell it down the road for a profit.

We had owned our business for a few years when we decided that it was time to explore the opportunity to sell. We had established a solid sales team and a name for ourselves in the affiliate marketing industry and were hitting revenue records year-over-year. We naively thought that our online company would be a hot commodity, and the offers would be lining up. What transpired from there were hard lessons and a heaping dose of reality.

Our first mistake was our choice of firm to represent us in an acquisition. To put it bluntly, we got suckered by the ol' bait and switch.

We were introduced to a firm through a close mutual friend and set up a meeting with a firm representative, a gentleman named Bruce. For that meeting, Bruce brought in a true ringer–an upper executive with their firm who knew our industry inside and out. He knew the lingo, he knew the players, and we had several mutual friends and colleagues in the business. We thought that with someone like that on our team, any concerns from a prospective buyer would be alleviated, and he'd be an asset in getting us the best deal. To be honest, we weren't overly impressed by Bruce or the rest of his team, but they really sold us on this ringer, and so we signed with that firm and looked forward to the process.

I'm sure you know what happened next.

After we signed with that firm, we never saw or heard from the ringer ever again. He'd been brought in to close *us* as opposed to helping us close *a buyer*. Bruce and his team became our day-to-day contacts, and the next several months proved frustrating and fruitless.

Typically, in that process you put together a presentation document of high-level information and numbers about your company, then prospective buyers are pitched using that document. Any party interested in exploring further and looking under the hood so to speak, signs a non-disclosure agreement (NDA) after which they become privy to more details and more confidential information. It's common to have dozens of prospective buyers sign an NDA to analyze the company further since the initial document is limited with respect to information. And yet during that entire process, I can count on one hand how many signed NDAs I received.

In fact, I ended up putting together my own list of potential strategic buyers after Bruce's team sent us a list of their prospects, and it left a lot to be desired. I wasn't sure if it was a matter of them not putting in the effort, or if their unfamiliarity with our industry left them in the dark.

Suffice to say we didn't sell. We didn't even get any letters of intent or go beyond the initial NDA process with anyone. Bruce was quick to explain that our business wasn't diverse enough and had no proprietary assets. He indicated that despite our big numbers with a small team and zero company debt, we weren't attractive to any buyer for the reasons he outlined. And not knowing any better, we believed him.

Over the next couple of years, we went to work trying to right the supposed wrongs that Bruce had indicated. We created new divisions to generate new diverse revenue streams, and we built (and acquired) some of our own tech to have proprietary assets. This is the main reason I created divisions in industries outside my wheelhouse like market research and mobile gaming and hired Riley and Myles respectively to oversee them. I did it because we had been led to believe that that's what we needed to do to sell the business.

All these moves cost money of course and impacted our profit levels compared to previous years. But with these new assets in place, we again explored the opportunity to sell.

This time we took on more meetings with more prospective firms looking to represent us and settled on a referral that we really connected with. They reviewed our books, saw how much higher our profits were prior to us undertaking those new opportunities as Bruce had urged us to do, and the first thing they said was, "Too bad you didn't reach out to us then, we could have sold you for more!"

They explained that even though diverse streams and proprietary assets are important, consistent growth year-over-year and an upward trend of annual profits were more attractive selling features, especially to a financial buyer intent on flipping the company in a few years to generate their own profits. All my partner and I could do was shake our heads and chalk it up to yet another life lesson.

Oh, and in case you're wondering, did we sell the second time? The answer is yes and no. We found a buyer. We signed a letter of intent. We agreed on a price and even a closing date. Then a couple of months before closing, our numbers inexplicably tanked, and the buyer backed out.

We found out that an employee had quietly created a competing business while on our payroll and shifted accounts over to his new entity during the COVID-19 pandemic. Well, that cost us our deal. That's another story for another day. But always remember this—money changes relationships. Gratitude, loyalty, even common human decency will be ignored by many people in favor of the almighty dollar. It's an unfortunate part of life and something I've learned the hard way on many occasions.

21
When the Money is No Longer Enough

YOU'VE HEARD THE SAYING, "MONEY ISN'T EVERYTHING." AND THAT is true, to a point.

In 2011 when I decided to leave my job and start my own business, my primary motivation was money.

Sure, self-employment comes with other benefits. You answer to only yourself, you set your own hours, you call the shots. But my main goal was to make a lot of money. In fact, I didn't have a passion for the affiliate marketing industry by that point, and in some ways I hated it if I'm being honest. But it was the easiest path for me to make a good living.

The first time I got a taste of real money was in 2008 when I worked at Incentaclick for my previous boss Sebastian. And in retrospect, after having spent several years with very little money, I just didn't know how to handle this newfound fortune.

I was single, in my early thirties, collecting five- and sometimes six-figure commission checks each month and traveling to industry trade shows all over the world. And for a little while, I let the money and the industry change me. I consumed too much alcohol, I was sometimes arrogant and careless, and I objectified women, even some in our office. I realize now that I got away with it because I was the top revenue generator and somewhat "untouchable" in the eyes of my co-workers.

One day I had too many drinks during a team lunch at a restaurant, and drunkenly yelled to one of my female colleagues across the table about how attractive I thought she was.

I've forgotten almost everything about that lunch now, but I do remember how silent everybody got, and I can imagine how uncomfortable that co-worker must have felt. Nobody was going to talk back to me because I was close to the boss and generated the most revenue. And in hindsight, maybe on some level I knew it. In fact, I recall another occasion when a co-worker told me that she hated how I always knew what was going on in the company before anyone else did. It was because I was close to management.

By the end of the day following that team lunch, I sobered up and realized how stupid I had been. It's like I had suddenly left my body and watched myself from above like an outside observer. I was embarrassed by my behavior and after that I flipped a switch—everything changed. I cut down on the alcohol, I became appreciative of my income instead of taking it for granted, and I tried to treat everyone at work with professionalism and respect.

I remember a short while later, a co-worker whom I was close to said to me, "You've changed, and *everybody* has noticed," and she meant that in a good way. My relationships with everyone improved, and my life improved with it.

By the end of 2009 I met a woman named Elsa on a Canadian online dating website called Lavalife. Five years later we got married, and in fact, 2014 was a big year for me—all in the same year, I got married, I turned forty, and we had our first child, our daughter Lilly. We went on to have a second baby, our son James Jr. in 2017. And I traded in bar nights, pitchers of beer, and industry trade shows for playgrounds, filtered water, and TV nights on the couch. I wouldn't have it any other way now.

Me and my wife Elsa on a gondola ride in Venice, Italy.

When I decided to create Fightful.com in 2016, I had owned my marketing company for about five years. The catalyst for launching that website was that I'd grown bored of an industry that I didn't love to begin with. We were doing well and making big money, but I didn't really care, because I didn't feel challenged or enthusiastic about my day-to-day professional life. I needed to do something different, something interesting, and something where money wasn't my main objective.

I don't live extravagantly aside from two things—my home, and my family vacations, both of which I do spend money on to provide the best quality of life for my wife and children. But money was not my incentive to create Fightful, and though it's become a profitable venture today, that was never the primary goal.

I'm from a small rural Canadian town with a population of about a thousand people. I grew up around farmland and the St. Lawrence River. I moved to the metropolis of Toronto when I was twenty-four years old to seek my fortune and a life that I didn't feel my hometown could provide. But as I got older, I developed a new appreciation for that small-town way of life, not to mention a disdain for the traffic and congestion that comes with being in a big city.

I bought my own small one-acre private island on the river back home in 2015 and renovated it with the intention of turning it into an investment cottage rental property. But two weeks a year we'd reserve time there for the family and the more often we went, the more I dreaded returning to the big city afterwards.

With the boys at my cottage. The previous owners named it Waterlily Island. My daughter's name is Lilly. I was destined to buy it!

Then in 2020 I had an epiphany after two major events happened in my life.

The first was the thing we all experienced—the COVID-19 pandemic—which forced me into home confinement for over a year. While I wasn't a big fan of being stuck in the house, I didn't miss going to the office at all, nor did I miss the traffic congestion in the surrounding area.

The second life event was the passing of my only sibling, my sister Sheri, at the age of forty-nine after a battle with cancer. Her death came less than two years after my father Cornelus passed at the age of eighty, also from cancer. But Sheri's passing really made me aware of my mortality and how short and fragile life really is. So, I decided that if I missed that small-town way of life, it was time to get back to it on a permanent basis.

My favorite family photo, and one of the last we ever took. My sister the late Sheri VanderLinden Gill is on the left, my dad the late Cor VanderLinden, my mom Tina, and me.

Before I even talked to my Toronto-born wife about my intentions, I first mapped out neighboring towns close enough to the city that she might go for my plan, but far enough away to leave the busyness behind. I was admittedly concerned that my wife wouldn't want to leave the city and that it would become a point of contention, so I wanted to make sure I had a plan. Then one day, she complained about traffic after dropping the kids off at school, and I knew the time was now. I revealed my plans, and she was fully on board.

When you know, you know. We found a three-acre piece of property in a town northeast of the big city and the moment we stepped out of our car we both loved it. It had a stream running through it and a pond full of fish. It was perfect. We bought that property to build our new home, then I sat down with my friend and partner, Luke, and told him that it was time for me to go. He wasn't at all surprised by that decision, and we worked out an agreement that saw me walk away from the day-to-day operations of an industry that I'd been involved with every day for almost twenty years. I told him that we could be doing a billion dollars a year in revenue, and it wouldn't have changed my mind. And I meant it.

How Much is Your Health Worth to You?

In the film *The Wrestler*, Mickey Rourke's character Randy "The Ram" Robinson defies doctor's orders not to wrestle again after suffering a heart attack in the locker room following a match. He did it because he needed the money, and he did it for the love of the only business he'd ever really known. In the final scene, he ascends to the top rope in a big match to deliver his devastating finishing move despite having felt the effects of another possible heart attack during the bout. Before he leaps, the screen fades to black, leaving viewers to wonder his fate.

I think we've all been there at one point. We don't exercise enough and the excuse is, we're too busy with work. We don't book that doctor's appointment that we've been intending to book, because we're too busy with work. We don't eat a healthy diet, or make enough time for our families, or for ourselves, because...I think you get it.

In the early 2000s when I was just establishing myself in the working world, I developed an autoimmune disorder called alopecia. In a nutshell, my immune system was out of whack and mistook my hair follicles as a threat and subsequently attacked them. It resulted in the loss of my facial hair and eyelashes, but for many years I kept it from overtaking my scalp with routine dermatologist appointments and steroid injections.

By 2020 the injections started becoming less effective, and circular bald patches started appearing and growing on my scalp. I had been told by my dermatologist that autoimmune disorders are often related to stress, and at that time I was juggling a busy work-life balance with forty employees and a young family at home so it isn't hard for me to understand what the source of that stress could have been.

I'd decided to leave my company because I didn't have a passion for the industry, and because the loss of immediate family made me aware of how short life is. But I also decided to leave so that I could free up time to work on myself, and my autoimmune issue.

I wrapped things up with my company in August of 2022. By that point, I had almost complete hair loss on my head. Knowing that exercise can serve as a stress reliever, I began a workout routine and as I write this almost a year later, I'm still consistent and disciplined in the gym five days a week. I also found a nutritionist and a naturopath to help me find the root cause of the issue, and I'm in the best physical shape of my life as I near the age of 50!

It took semi-retirement for all of that to happen. And I realize not everyone has that luxury. But I could have done these things while I worked in the office full-time, I just didn't. It wasn't until I lost my sister that I became more cognizant of my own mortality and motivated to work on me. And in retrospect, I can't believe it took me almost twenty years to take a deep dive into my autoimmunity!

Don't do what I did. If you have any health concerns, take care of it. Don't put it off until tomorrow, because tomorrow could turn into five years and you might regret procrastinating. A day consists of twenty-four hours, so there's always time for you to take care of you.

Oh and in case you're curious–as I write this I'm still bald, but I'm starting to see some regrowth, and I have a much better understanding of my gut health than I did when I started!

So, what's my point to all this?

Look, financial independence is a blessing. Not having to live paycheck to paycheck, not having to worry about your mortgage, or your retirement, if nothing else just for your peace of mind alone, is a blessing. All the decisions that I've made over the years and all the risks that I took, got me to a good place and I feel very fortunate. And if any of the stories that I've told in this book help you, whether at your job, or starting your own business, or helping your existing business succeed, that's great! That was my objective in the first place.

But I guess my point is happiness is not about that new Ferrari. It's not about that new Rolex or a trip to Europe. We live in a social media world in which we're influenced by people that do nothing but show off those material possessions and a lavish lifestyle all day, and for many of us that becomes the dream, and those people become our heroes. Well guess what? In many instances, those people don't own those items. It's an illusion designed to fit their narrative and create whatever perception they want to convey online.

Family, health, peace of mind—that is what happiness means to me. And yes, financial independence has helped me get there.

Whatever happiness means to you, I hope you achieve it, and I hope that somehow, some way, this book helps you get there, even if only a little!

Otherwise, if you like a good story, hopefully one of mine appealed to you.

My Proudest Achievements

Often when a celebrity or business tycoon is asked in interviews about their proudest achievement, the common answer will be that they bought their mother a house, or they paid off a family member's mortgage. My own answer is subsequently not original but I'm proud of the fact that I got to do something similar not once, but twice.

In the spring of 2016, my parents were months away from their respective seventy-eighth birthdays. It was becoming harder and harder for my mother to maintain the house and yard of the property where they'd lived for over twenty years, and so they decided it was time to sell and downsize. My parents then moved in with my sister Sheri and her husband Ron as a stopgap before buying a new place.

This was the end of an era for my family—my parents' home with the "Sold" sign on it.

About a year later, in May of 2017, they were still living at my sister's house. And even though my mom and dad were beloved and respected by Sheri and Ron, I think they missed their privacy, and Ron definitely missed being able to commandeer the television at night! So, I sat down with my parents to discuss their game plan.

My father didn't see the point of spending money at his age to buy a new house. He was basically waited on hand and foot and was content with his situation. My mother felt the opposite; she felt like a burden on my sister. But unless Dad would agree to buy, she was stuck. So, I decided to step in, and I feel so fortunate to this day that I could.

I called a family meeting with my parents as well as Sheri and Ron and told them that I had a solution—I would buy Mom and Dad a house. That way my sister would get her privacy back, and my dad wouldn't have to spend any money. I found them a modest bungalow just around the corner from my sister's house, and I'm proud to say that my father spent the rest of his life happy and comfortable in his own environment.

The second story took place the same year, 2017. My wife was very close to her grandparents, who had lived in the same old house in downtown Toronto for over forty years. By this point her grandparents were in their eighties, and the house was badly in need of repair. To make matters worse, some of the grandparents' children were pressuring them to be put on the title of the house, and the stress and frustration was causing Grandpa to consider selling to rid himself of the family headaches.

Two of their children also lived in the home and paid minimal rent, and I'd been told that one of them commonly short-paid his parents despite having his wife and two young children living there with him. I also discovered that even though they'd lived there for so many years, the grandparents had taken out a six-figure mortgage to help some of their children financially.

Grandma would speak to my wife in tears, fearful that Grandpa would sell and that they would have nowhere to go, since that house had been their only home since immigrating to Canada from Trinidad decades prior. So I came up with an idea, and I called a meeting with my wife, my wife's mother Margaret—the grandparents' oldest child, who cared deeply for the well-being of her mom and dad—and the grandparents' oldest son, Clive. I then proposed a solution—I would buy the house anonymously, complete a full renovation, and then allow the grandparents to live there rent-free for the rest of their lives.

The plan would go like this: Clive would tell his parents that he was approached by an investor friend who was interested in the property, but he understood the owners to be an elderly couple who had lived there for years, and so he wanted to do right by them. My real estate agent then came up with a fair valuation based on comparables in that area, and Clive presented the offer to them. They were ecstatic to get the offer and accepted, and moved in with Clive temporarily while the house was renovated, after which they moved back into their newly remodeled home.

Upon the completion of the renovation, I told Clive and Margaret that their one brother who had lived there previously could return, because I wanted someone to help the grandparents. But I felt it was for the best that the other brother find his own accommodations for himself and his family, and so the offer to return was not extended to him. The grandparents' newfound wealth caused a host of new problems, however, because some of their children took advantage of them and got access to a lot of that money. I've said it many times—money changes relationships.

Ultimately, members of the family discovered that I was the one who bought the house. And I guess in retrospect it was obvious. One cousin told me plainly one day, "When someone comes out of nowhere and offers my grandparents that kind of a deal, who else could it be? It had to be you." Several members of the family thanked me for the gesture and expressed their appreciation. But I did it for Grandma, for Grandpa, for Margaret, and for my wife.

REFERENCES

Affairs, Office of Public. 2012. "Bank Agrees to Enhanced Compliance Obligations, Oversight by Monitorin Connection with Five-year Agreement." *Office of Public Affairs - U.S. Department of Justice.* December 11. https://www.justice.gov/opa/pr/hsbc-holdings-plc-and-hsbc-bank-usa-na-admit-anti-money-laundering-and-sanctions-violations.

Ault, Susanne. 2014. *Survey: YouTube Stars More Popular Than Mainstream Celebs Among U.S. Teens.* August 5. https://variety.com/2014/digital/news/survey-youtube-stars-more-popular-than-mainstream-celebs-among-u-s-teens-1201275245/.

Caporal, Jack. 2022. *Average American Household Debt in 2023: Facts and Figures.* September 20. https://www.fool.com/the-ascent/research/average-household-debt/.

Cayasso, José. 2022. *The Real Numbers Behind Shark Tank.* August 19. https://slidebean.com/blog/the-real-numbers-behind-shark-tank.

Emes, Claire. 2017. *In Brief: The Changing Role Of Women?* May. https://www.ipsos.com/sites/default/files/2017-05/global_trends.pdf.

Fermie, Etienne. 2020. *How Evander Holyfield won and lost his £240m fortune after dodgy business deals led to eviction from 109-room mansion.* August 11. https://www.thesun.co.uk/sport/12371134/evander-holyfield-lost-fortune-business/.

Fishkin, Rand. 2018. *2018 Search Market Share: Myths vs. Realities of Google, Bing, Amazon, Facebook, DuckDuckGo, & More*. October 16. https://sparktoro.com/blog/2018-search-market-share-myths-vs-realities-of-google-bing-amazon-facebook-duckduckgo-more/.

Fontevecchia, Agustino. 2012. *HSBC Helped Terrorists, Iran, Mexican Drug Cartels Launder Money, Senate Report Says*. July 16. https://www.forbes.com/sites/afontevecchia/2012/07/16/hsbc-helped-terrorists-iran-mexican-drug-cartels-launder-money-senate-report-says.

Frankel, Michelle Black and Robin Saks. 2023. *What Is The Average Credit Card Interest Rate This Week?* August 28. https://www.forbes.com/advisor/credit-cards/average-credit-card-interest-rate/.

Goel, Vindu. 2017. *Verizon Completes $4.48 Billion Purchase of Yahoo, Ending an Era*. June 13. https://www.nytimes.com/2017/06/13/technology/yahoo-verizon-marissa-mayer.html.

Howarth, Josh. 2023. *Startup Failure Rate Statistics (2023)*. March 16. https://explodingtopics.com/blog/startup-failure-stats.

Johnson, Mike. 2008. *LATEST ON WWE LAWSUIT OVER AWA NAME: DALE GAGNER ORDERED TO PAY WWE COURT FEES AFTER NOT RESPONDING TO COURT MANDATES*. April 15. https://www.pwinsider.com/ViewArticle.php?id=30452&p=1.

Kemp, Simon. 2020. *Digital 2020: Global Digital Overview*. January 30. https://datareportal.com/reports/digital-2020-global-digital-overview.

Reichel, Mark. 2007. *WWE Sues Gagner for AWA Trademark Infringement*. April 27. http://dailydoseofip.blogspot.com/2007/04/wwe-sues-gagner-for-awa-trademark.html.

Rooney, Ben. 2015. *https://www.nytimes.com/2017/06/13/ technology/yahoo-verizon-marissa-mayer.html.* May 12. https://money.cnn.com/2015/05/12/investing/verizon-buys-aol/index.html.

Ruby, Daniel. 2023. *139 SEO Statistics for 2023 (Current State & Trends).* August 9. https://www.demandsage.com/seo-statistics/.

Schawbel, Dan. 2018. *Survey: Remote Workers Are More Disengaged and More Likely to Quit.* November 15. https://hbr.org/2018/11/survey-remote-workers-are-more-disengaged-and-more-likely-to-quit.

Smith, Robert W, Isobel Barnes, Jane Green, Gillian K Reeves, Valerie Beral, and Sarah and Floud. 2021. *Social isolation and risk of heart disease and stroke: analysis of two large UK prospective studies.* March 2. https://www.ncbi.nlm.nih.gov/pmc/articles/PMC7994247/.

ACKNOWLEDGMENTS

I'VE ALWAYS BEEN A STORYTELLER. IT'S A TRAIT I PICKED UP FROM my father. I never thought having the ability to think of a relevant story from personal experience to match a topic of conversation would ever be of value, and yet here we are! Dad was also the businessman of the family, and during my childhood he always had a hand in various endeavors and never worked for anyone else. And so, my entrepreneurial spirit came from him as well. This book probably wouldn't be possible had I not inherited these attributes from the late Cornelus VanderLinden, who told me many stories for many years, sometimes repeatedly! I think of him often, and I miss him.

I'm eternally grateful for my mother, Tina VanderLinden. Everybody says that their mom is the best, but mine really is! She always supported me in everything I wanted to do, even when that meant moving from a small town to the big city all alone or leaving a stable job to run a pro wrestling website. She is the kindest, most unselfish, and most considerate person I've ever known, and I can only hope to have as positive an impact on the people in my life as she has had on the people around her. She means everything to me, and I hope she knows that.

My sister, the late Sheri VanderLinden Gill, was my mentor growing up and my rock. She was the organized one who always made sure that everything got done right and on time. And she was the social butterfly who kept in touch with family members near and far, a skill I'm embarrassed to say I have yet to master. My quick wit and sharp tongue were developed as a sort of defense mechanism, because I had to try to keep up with her! But despite her humor and sarcasm, she was the one I would call when I had a problem—especially if I had been the one to cause it—because she would offer advice without passing judgment or berating me over my mistakes. She's been gone for several years, and some days I still can't believe it.

To my sister's husband, my brother-in-law, Ron Gill, who unexpectedly became a caregiver and displayed nothing but strength and patience on the outside even while I know he was hurting on the inside. After Sheri's passing, I sort of volunteered Ron as the "fix-it guy"; if Mom needs something, Ron will handle it. If there's a problem with the cottage, Ron will handle it. I don't say it enough, but I appreciate him, and maybe we're not blood, but we are family.

My favorite teacher of all time was my high school history teacher, Mr. Hall. I was the kind of student who got good grades if I pushed myself, but at that time I wasn't motivated by school, and so I rarely took notes or read the textbooks and coasted to just passable grades. I would sometimes joke around in class or make sarcastic remarks. And that's why I loved Mr. Hall. He figured out how to get my attention by throwing my nonsense right back at me. My best memory is when he asked the class a question that had multiple answers. At the time, the chalkboard was completely blank. I answered first, and he wrote my answer in tiny letters in the bottom right corner of the empty board. Everyone laughed and so did I. I loved it. Mr. Hall taught me that there's no generic solution to keep every person engaged and to find out what makes each person tick.

To my boss from Incentaclick, "Sebastian". He was the first employer to ever put his trust and faith in me to the point that he not only gave me the freedom to close and manage my own deals, but he would confide in me and ask my opinion on issues related to the general operations of the company. His openness provided me with a free education on running a business, and I'll forever remember his kindness, his sense of humor, and his generosity. Years after we both left that company, we always kept in touch, and I still smile when I think about the time at a client dinner when he proclaimed that he was making me an honorary Jew! I love the guy.

To everyone I've ever worked with who helped me along the way in the business world: co-workers, colleagues, and employees. I won't name names so that I don't leave anyone out, but those I was closest to and whose work I valued most, you know who you are. Thank you.

Thanks to my buddy and accounting wizard Craig for helping me get the details right on the corporate tax related stuff and making me sound like I know what I'm talking about!

Twenty years ago, I wouldn't have predicted that I would someday own a multimillion-dollar business alongside my friend Luke. We went from those morning breakfasts at Yahoo to that infamous Yahoo lunch, to lots of shenanigans at AZ Ads and Incentaclick, to somehow becoming husbands, fathers, and competent businesspeople. You know me better than just about anyone, and the fact that our friendship has endured the ups and downs of the affiliate marketing business while so many other friendships were permanently dismantled by that industry speaks volumes. Thanks, buddy.

I've had the good fortune of maintaining the same friendships for decades. Wayne, Chatty, Kelvin, Luke, Vettraino, Russ, Billy—sometimes life gets in the way, and we don't get to see each other as often as we wish, but when we do, it's like not a single day has passed. I love you guys.

I'm saving the best for last—to my wife, Elsa, and my children, Lilly and Jimmy. I don't know why, but I've always had a problem saying the words, "I love you," and so with my kids I always say, "Daddy loves you," instead. But Elsa is the backbone of our family, and I love her immensely. She's a wonderful mother, one hell of a great cook, and a supportive wife who backs me in every decision I make, including my decision to leave our home city for a new life in a small town. At times, I know Elsa feels undervalued or underappreciated, because I've always been the moneymaker. But it was only because of her taking care of everything at home that I had the time and opportunity to take care of everything financially. I don't say it enough, but I appreciate you, and I thank you. And Lilly and Jimmy—Daddy is so proud of you guys. You are both so smart and so funny. You have both blossomed before my eyes, and I'm trying to soak it all in and enjoy it while you're still small, before those teenage years have you wanting nothing to do with me for a while! You both are destined to do great in life, but when times are tough, don't forget that I'll always be there for you. Daddy loves you.

ABOUT THE AUTHOR

JAMES VANDERLINDEN, KNOWN ONLINE AS Jimmy Van, is a business owner, content creator, writer, and podcaster. His previous publishing credits include a memoir about his experiences in professional wrestling entitled *Wrestling's Underbelly: From Bingo Halls to Shopping Malls,* as well as a feature in the *Hamilton Spectator* newspaper about the passing of pro wrestler Owen Hart in 1999. Today he does podcasts and occasionally writes features for his web platform Fightful.com (with almost three million monthly views, 100,000+ YouTube subscribers and 160,000+ Meta (Twitter) followers). He also founded a non-profit, GrapplingwithGrief.com, inspired by the passing of his father and sister. VanderLinden lives in Toronto, Canada, with his wife and two children.

www.ingramcontent.com/pod-product-compliance
Lightning Source LLC
Chambersburg PA
CBHW030932180526
45163CB00002B/538